The Why Behind the Buy

*Connect With Your
Customers Before You Sell*

Philip Masiello

Copyright page

(Enter text here)

ISBN: 979-8-9882053-2-6

Appsydo, LLC

Contents

Preface

Selling to consumers today is more complex than ever. The strategies that worked a decade ago are outdated, and brands that fail to evolve quickly find themselves struggling to keep up. With consumers bombarded by messages across multiple platforms, social media, connected TV, search engines, and eCommerce marketplaces, the challenge isn't just capturing attention but creating meaningful connections that drive loyalty and sales.

As the founder of CrunchGrowth Revenue Acceleration Agency, I have spent years mastering this evolving landscape. With over 30 years of experience marketing to consumers, I've witnessed the industry's transformation from traditional print and television advertising to the highly segmented, data-driven world we operate in today. I've launched and scaled multiple eCommerce businesses, built disruptive brands, and learned firsthand what it takes to win in an increasingly digital world.

Through CrunchGrowth, we've helped brands of all sizes, from startups to established enterprises, scale faster, improve customer engagement, and maximize revenue. Whether it's Connected TV advertising, online performance marketing, or social selling, our agency has been at the forefront of helping businesses break through the noise and reach consumers where they are.

This book is a culmination of over three decades of insights, failures, and successes, a guide to understanding today's consumer, leveraging the right marketing channels, and executing strategies that drive real, sustainable growth. If you want to sell smarter, scale faster, and build stronger customer relationships, this book will show you how.

"The Why Behind the Buy: Connecting With Your Customers Before Selling To Them"

This book is an essential guide for companies navigating today's consumer-driven landscape, where the power has shifted to buyers, and trust, authenticity, and customer experience are the new currencies of success.

What makes this book unique is its comprehensive exploration of the mistakes businesses make when trying to sell to increasingly skeptical consumers. More importantly, it offers practical, actionable solutions to build genuine connections that lead to long-term loyalty. This book is not just about selling products; it's about understanding the complete customer journey, from discovery to loyalty, and creating meaningful, lasting relationships.

The book directly addresses the challenges faced by marketers, business owners, and brand managers, including standing out in a saturated market, dealing with skeptical buyers, and navigating modern marketing platforms like social media and eCommerce marketplaces. Its unique value lies in aligning sales efforts with the values and expectations of today's consumers, offering clear strategies to overcome these challenges and build lasting relationships.

After reading this book, readers will be equipped to effectively engage with their customers by focusing on authentic branding, delivering exceptional user experiences, and using data-driven insights to personalize their marketing strategies. They'll learn how to turn one-time buyers into loyal advocates, develop sustainable marketing approaches that prioritize long-term growth, and navigate the complexities of selling on platforms like Amazon while maintaining their brand identity. Ultimately, readers will walk away with actionable tactics to build a brand that truly matters to their customers, not just for the moment but for the long haul.

Introduction

It takes approximately 7.5 hours of content consumption for a prospective customer to build enough trust in a brand to make a meaningful buying decision.

The Age of the Empowered Consumer

We live in a time when the power dynamic between brands and consumers has fundamentally shifted. Digital platforms have democratized information, transforming how products are marketed and sold. No longer are brands the gatekeepers of information, controlling narratives and dictating engagement. Today, consumers are more informed, connected, and discerning than ever, thanks to the rise of social media, online marketplaces, and peer-driven content.

The Power Shift: From Brands to Consumers

This shift has profound implications for businesses, requiring them to rethink their marketing strategies and customer engagement. In the past, consumers had limited access to product information. Advertising and branding dominated public perception, and companies had the upper hand in influencing purchasing decisions. That model no longer applies. Today, with just a few clicks, consumers can research products, read reviews, watch unboxing videos, and compare pricing in minutes. They are no longer passive recipients of brand messaging but active participants in the buying process.

Take Amazon, for example, where customer reviews often carry more weight than a brand's marketing campaign. According to a 2022 PowerReviews survey, 93% of consumers read online reviews before making a purchase. This statistic highlights how influence has shifted from companies to the customers using their products. Consumers now drive conversations, expose product flaws, and advocate for brands they trust.

Another example is the beauty industry, where brands like Glossier have thrived by prioritizing community engagement over traditional top-down marketing. Glossier has cultivated a loyal following by actively listening to its customers and developing products based on their feedback. This brand evolution underscores a crucial point: consumers now decide which products succeed and which fade into obscurity.

The End of the Product-First Strategy

For decades, many businesses operated under the assumption that a high-quality product alone would attract customers. However, in the age of the empowered consumer, this approach is no longer enough. Modern buyers seek more than just good products; they want meaningful connections with brands. The buying journey has evolved from a simple transaction into a multi-layered experience where trust, authenticity, and shared values play a pivotal role.

Consider the shift in consumer expectations regarding sustainability. Patagonia, a brand known for its commitment to environmental causes, has positioned itself as a leader in outdoor apparel not just because of its products but because of its dedication to sustainability. A survey by Accenture found that 63% of global consumers prefer to buy from companies that reflect their values and beliefs. Patagonia's success comes from selling a vision of environmental responsibility, not just jackets.

These examples underscore a new reality: today's consumers expect brands to have a purpose beyond profit. The product-first strategy must give way to a customer-centric approach, where engagement, transparency, and shared values take center stage.

Authenticity and Transparency: The New Currency

Modern consumers crave authenticity. In an era of easy access to information, disingenuous marketing or misleading claims are quickly exposed. Consumers can verify a brand's promises and, through social media, amplify their voices if they feel deceived. Companies that fail to meet expectations risk not only losing customers but also facing public backlash.

Consider how "cancel culture" has impacted brands. Victoria's Secret, for example, has faced intense scrutiny and declining sales due to a perceived disconnect between its brand messaging and shifting consumer values. On the other hand, brands like Everlane, which champions "radical transparency" by openly sharing production processes and cost breakdowns, have built trust and loyalty by staying true to their values. Everlane's commitment to honesty resonates with consumers who are skeptical of hidden motives.

This desire for authenticity also explains the rapid rise of influencer marketing. Consumers trust recommendations from individuals they follow online more than traditional advertisements. However, as consumers become more discerning, the emphasis has shifted to "micro-influencers", those with smaller but highly engaged audiences, who are perceived as more relatable and trustworthy than high-profile influencers who may appear detached or commercially driven.

The New Paradigm of Consumer Empowerment

The era of the empowered consumer has redefined what it means to be a successful brand. The rise of e-commerce, social media, and digital marketplaces has granted consumers unprecedented control over the buying process. This shift allows them to discover, evaluate, and purchase products on their own terms. The brands that prioritize transparency, authenticity, and engagement will thrive in this new landscape.

In the following chapters, we will explore the intricate dynamics of this power shift, examining how businesses can adapt to meet the expectations of a more discerning, empowered consumer. From redefining marketing strategies to building trust through transparency, this book will serve as a roadmap for success in a world where consumers are in control. The old rules no longer apply, and brands that fail to evolve will inevitably be left behind. But for those willing to embrace this new reality, the opportunities are limitless.

Understanding Generational Differences

To engage effectively with their audience, businesses must understand the generational differences shaping consumer behavior. Millennials, Gen Z, Gen X, and Baby Boomers each have distinct attitudes, values, and expectations influenced by their unique experiences. These differences impact how they interact with brands, make purchasing decisions, and use digital platforms. Recognizing and adapting to these generational nuances is crucial for any brand seeking to build meaningful and lasting customer relationships.

Gen Z Consumers (Born 1997–2012)

Gen Z, the first generation to grow up fully immersed in digital technology, has even higher expectations for transparency, inclusivity, and digital fluency. As an emerging force in consumer spending, they represent a crucial demographic for businesses looking to adapt to the future of commerce.

1. **Hyper-Awareness and Activism**: Gen Z is highly socially and politically aware. Brands perceived as inauthentic or failing to meet ethical commitments face swift backlash. Fast fashion brands, for instance, have struggled with Gen Z's sustainability focus, prompting companies like H&M to introduce eco-friendly product lines.

2. **Digital Natives and Short Attention Spans**: Growing up in an era of information overload has shortened Gen Z's attention span. Brands must engage them quickly and meaningfully through bite-sized content, such as Instagram stories, TikTok videos, or Snapchat ads.

3. **Authenticity and Transparency as Baseline Expectations**: Authenticity is not just valued, it is expected. Gen Z consumers are highly skilled at detecting inauthenticity. Companies like Glossier have succeeded by prioritizing transparency and community involvement, making customers feel like insiders rather than mere buyers.

4. **Diverse Representation and Inclusivity**: Gen Z demands that brands reflect the diversity of the world around them. Fenty Beauty set a new industry standard by launching with 40 foundation shades, proving that inclusivity is not optional but a necessity for brand relevance.

Millennial Consumers (Born 1981–1996)

Millennials, often called the first "digital natives," are among the most influential drivers of the empowered consumer movement. Having grown up during the rise of the internet and social media, their approach to discovering, evaluating, and purchasing products has been profoundly shaped by digital connectivity. Several key traits define Millennials' consumption behavior:

1. **Value-Driven Purchasing**: Millennials support brands that reflect their values, particularly in social justice, environmental sustainability, and ethical business practices. Brands like TOMS and Warby Parker gained popularity due to their "buy one, give one" business models, aligning with Millennials' desire to see their purchases contribute to a greater cause.

2. **Experience Over Product**: This generation prioritizes experiences over material goods. Brands like Airbnb and Uber

have thrived by offering services that create memorable experiences rather than simply delivering products. Businesses must create immersive, engaging brand experiences that go beyond mere transactions.

3. **Skepticism Toward Traditional Advertising**: Millennials are less likely to trust traditional advertising. Instead, they rely on peer reviews, influencer recommendations, and social media engagement. Brands that fail to connect authentically or appear overly corporate risk alienating this audience.

4. **Personalization and Customization**: Millennials appreciate brands that offer tailored experiences. Platforms like Spotify and Netflix, which customize content based on individual preferences, have set the standard for personalized marketing and product recommendations.

Generation X Consumers (Born 1965–1980)

Often overlooked in consumer discussions, Gen X plays a vital role in the marketplace. Many are in their peak earning years, making them a powerful demographic with significant spending power.

1. **Brand Loyalty**: Unlike younger generations, Gen X tends to be more brand-loyal, particularly to companies they have trusted for years. However, they will switch if brands fail to meet modern standards of convenience, value, or digital integration.

2. **A Preference for Practicality**: Gen X is pragmatic and price-conscious. While they appreciate digital shopping tools, they are less swayed by trends and brand personalities than Millennials or Gen Z. Value-driven offers, rewards programs, and straightforward advertising resonate most with them.

3. **Growing Comfort with Digital Platforms**: Though not digital natives, Gen X has embraced e-commerce and social media for product discovery. However, they still value in-person experiences,

often preferring a hybrid shopping model that combines online convenience with in-store interactions.

4. **Skepticism Toward Online Reviews**: While younger generations rely heavily on peer reviews, Gen X tends to be more skeptical. They seek validation from multiple sources before purchasing, making clear, consistent, and trustworthy brand messaging essential.

Baby Boomers (Born 1946–1964)

Although Baby Boomers are less digitally inclined than younger consumers, their preferences still hold significant market influence, especially in industries like healthcare, travel, and home goods.

1. **Traditional Shopping Preferences**: Many Baby Boomers prefer shopping in physical stores. However, this behavior has shifted post-pandemic as they become more comfortable with e-commerce. Providing seamless in-store experiences with digital conveniences, such as mobile payments or curbside pickup, can enhance their engagement.

2. **Desire for Simplicity and Reliability**: Boomers value clear communication, ease of use, and dependable customer service. Unlike Millennials and Gen Z, they are less influenced by trends and more focused on product quality and reliability.

3. **Health and Wellness Focus**: Baby Boomers prioritize health and wellness, making them receptive to brands that cater to aging-related concerns, from supplements to fitness products. Loyalty programs and discounts also appeal to their preference for value and trust.

Navigating Generational Shifts in Consumer Empowerment

Each generation brings unique expectations and behaviors to the marketplace, requiring businesses to tailor their strategies accordingly.

Millennials and Gen Z push brands toward greater transparency, authenticity, and value alignment, while Gen X and Baby Boomers focus more on reliability, simplicity, and practical value.

In the age of the empowered consumer, understanding and responding to generational differences is essential for building strong, lasting relationships across all demographics. Brands that embrace this complexity and adapt their strategies will be best positioned to thrive in the evolving consumer landscape.

Chapter 1

The Rise Of
The Savvy Consumer

The Evolution of Consumer Behavior

In the 1980s and 1990s, shopping was a straightforward process. Consumers walked into stores, browsed the aisles, and made purchasing decisions based largely on advertisements or word-of-mouth recommendations from family and friends. There was little opportunity for deeper investigation. Brands held the power, shaping narratives through polished ads and eye-catching packaging. If your brand had a television presence or a high-profile endorsement, you had a significant advantage. Consumers simply followed.

Fast-forward to today, and the landscape has shifted dramatically. The rise of the internet, social media, and e-commerce has fundamentally changed the game, empowering consumers like never before. Blind trust in a brand's message is a thing of the past. Today's buyers are informed, cautious, and savvier than ever.

The Power of Information

Consider Emily, a typical 30-something consumer searching for a new vacuum cleaner. In the past, she might have visited her local department store, chosen a sleek Dyson model based on a TV commercial she saw the night before, and made the purchase on the spot. That's no longer how Emily, or most consumers, shop.

Instead, she opens her laptop and types "best vacuums for pet hair" into Google. Instantly, she's presented with dozens of comparison articles, YouTube video reviews, and user-generated content from fellow pet owners struggling with fur-covered floors.

Emily watches a well-known home blogger put three different vacuum models through rigorous testing, highlighting their pros and cons. She reads dozens of Amazon reviews, scanning for key phrases like "long battery life" and "easy to clean." She even checks the brands' social media pages to see how they handle customer complaints.

Before she ever sets foot in a store, or clicks "Buy Now", Emily has thoroughly analyzed every aspect of her purchase, armed with research and validation from other consumers. This research-driven buying process is the new reality for brands: they are no longer the sole voice influencing the consumer. Buyers have millions of other voices to consult, and they do.

The Role of Social Media and Reviews

Now, imagine John, an avid outdoorsman in his early 40s searching for a new hiking backpack. Instead of browsing the aisles of a sporting goods store, he's scrolling through Instagram, watching influencers test gear in real-world conditions.

In today's marketplace, where authenticity outweighs polished marketing, John values a YouTube or Instagram review from an outdoor expert far more than a traditional ad campaign. He takes note when an influencer he trusts mentions that a particular backpack has endured months of grueling hikes. This new form of word-of-mouth marketing is raw, real, and incredibly persuasive.

Social proof has become a driving force in modern consumerism. People no longer trust brands at face value, they trust the experiences of others who have already made the purchase. Reviews, testimonials, and user-generated content (UGC) hold more credibility than traditional advertising because they come from real people with no apparent agenda.

The impact of this shift is undeniable:

- **92% of consumers trust recommendations from friends and family over any form of advertising.**
- **Even strangers on the internet hold more sway than polished corporate messaging.**
- **A single negative review or viral complaint can unravel a multi-million-dollar ad campaign.**

Brands that once controlled the message must now navigate an unfiltered feedback loop where every customer interaction is public, reviewed, and shared across multiple platforms. John's trust in a backpack brand will be built not on how the company markets itself but on the social proof provided by fellow outdoor enthusiasts and influencers.

Case Study: Graza's Rapid Growth

A question we often hear from clients: **"How did Graza scale so quickly?"**

Graza's journey is a masterclass in branding, positioning, and execution. We break down the exact steps they used, starting with finding their place in the **Better and Different** quadrant

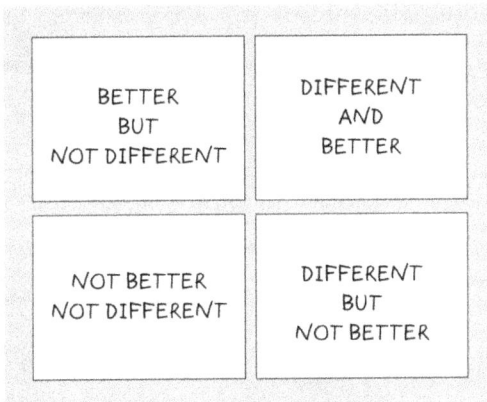

BETTER BUT NOT DIFFERENT	DIFFERENT AND BETTER
NOT BETTER NOT DIFFERENT	DIFFERENT BUT NOT BETTER

Graza didn't just aim to be better; they focused on being different. They took high-quality olive oil, packaged it in a fresh, convenient way, and made the use case crystal clear: one for cooking, one for dressing.

The Key Strategies Behind Graza's Success:

1. **Unique Product Concept** – Founders Andrew Benin and Allen Dushi introduced premium olive oil that was fun and accessible, targeting Millennials and Gen Z.
2. **Innovative Packaging** – They chose squeeze bottles in vibrant green, making olive oil easy and enjoyable to use.
3. **Product Differentiation** – Graza launched two products: "Drizzle" (finishing oil) and "Sizzle" (cooking oil), each tailored to specific culinary needs.
4. **Direct-to-Consumer (DTC) Launch** – They built a strong online presence to engage directly with customers and streamline the shopping experience.
5. **Influencer Marketing** – Graza seeded over 300 influencer kits, generating buzz before the official launch. Their organic, no-strings-attached approach led to authentic, engaging content across social platforms.
6. **Retail Expansion** – After gaining traction online, Graza strategically partnered with Whole Foods and Foxtrot to broaden its reach.
7. **Social Media Engagement** – From early social engagement to influencer seeding and retail collaborations, every marketing effort focused on standing out and connecting personally with customers.

Too often, brands get stuck in traditional tactics that no longer work. Graza's success reminds us that **being different** is what grabs attention. Growth comes from thinking creatively, taking risks, and genuinely engaging with your audience.

Why Brands Get It Wrong

Despite the drastic shift in consumer behavior, many brands still rely on outdated tactics. They bombard consumers with aggressive ads, assuming that more exposure equates to more sales. They expect customers to make purchases based on slogans and jingles rather than conducting thorough research.

One of the biggest mistakes companies make today is underestimating the effort involved in a consumer's decision-making process. It's no longer enough to simply put a product in front of a potential buyer and expect brand recognition to do the work. Consumers like Emily and John demand proof, not promises.

Even large brands sometimes fail to grasp the depth of the research phase. Companies may invest millions in developing the perfect product, only to watch it fail because they neglected to engage with the online communities that could have validated or critiqued it before launch. In today's market, ignoring consumer dialogue is a fatal error.

Take, for example, Citizen's launch of an innovative smartwatch. The company was confident that its technical specifications and sleek design would be enough to attract consumers.

However, they overlooked the growing criticism on social media about the watch's short battery life and clunky interface, issues that surfaced weeks before launch. Negative reviews flooded Amazon, influencers quickly pivoted to more user-friendly alternatives, and within months, the product was pulled from the market, becoming a cautionary tale.

Adapting to the New Consumer

To thrive in this new reality, brands must shift their approach. Every stage of the customer journey, from the first exposure to post-purchase experience, is filled with opportunities for either connection or failure.

Success today depends on being part of the conversation. Brands must go where their consumers are, whether on Reddit, Instagram, or niche Facebook groups, and actively listen. Understanding the research process, acknowledging consumer skepticism, and addressing concerns upfront is key to building trust. The modern consumer can spot a marketing gimmick from miles away; their loyalty must be earned, not bought.

The rise of the savvy consumer has fundamentally changed the rules of selling. A great product alone is no longer enough. Brands must demonstrate why they can be trusted, what others think of them, and how they respond to consumer needs.

In this landscape, ignoring the power of the informed consumer is a recipe for irrelevance. Successful brands will embrace this shift, respect the research phase, and recognize that consumers now hold all the cards. Whether it's Emily choosing her next vacuum or John selecting his ideal hiking backpack, the purchase journey is no longer straightforward, it's filled with reviews, comparisons, and critiques. Brands that fail to engage with this journey risk being left behind.

Consumer Psychology: The Informed Skeptic

The relationship between brands and consumers has evolved dramatically over the last few decades. While consumers once followed brand messaging without question, today's buyers are skeptical, demanding, and thoroughly informed before making a purchase.

Why has skepticism become the norm? The answer lies in the sheer availability of information and the over-saturation of marketing messages. The average person encounters thousands of ads, emails, and promotional campaigns daily, from billboards to Instagram feeds. The more exposure consumers have to these messages, the more discerning they become about which ones to trust.

Modern consumers have become experts at filtering out noise and focusing on authenticity. The rise of fake news, misleading advertising, and corporate scandals has made them more cautious. They no longer take a brand's promises at face value; they seek evidence, proof, and transparency.

This skepticism is driven by several key psychological factors:

- **Loss of Trust in Institutions:** Over the years, corporate scandals and unethical practices have eroded consumer confidence. Whether it's Volkswagen's emissions scandal, Facebook's data privacy breaches, or brands exaggerating their environmental impact, these incidents have contributed to widespread distrust in large corporations.

- **The Empowerment of Information:** With unlimited information at their fingertips, consumers no longer rely on a single source for product knowledge. They check reviews, compare competitors, and seek firsthand user experiences that challenge a brand's polished message. This empowerment makes them less likely to accept marketing claims without validation.

- **The Illusion of Choice:** While consumers have more options than ever, this paradoxically makes them more selective. Given 20 similar choices for a single product, they will invest more time researching the best option. This deep engagement in the research phase means consumers scrutinize everything, from product descriptions to corporate values.

In this environment, trust has become the most valuable currency for brands. The modern consumer seeks companies that align with their values, provide transparent information, and demonstrate genuine care for their customers. Brands that prioritize honesty, engage authentically, and respect the intelligence of their audience will be the ones that succeed in the evolving marketplace.

Social Proof: The New Marketing Force

While consumer psychology is one piece of the puzzle, another equally important factor is the reliance on social proof. In an age where peer reviews, influencer endorsements, and user-generated content carry more weight than brand advertisements, social proof can make or break a product's success.

Let's take a closer look at how different forms of social proof influence buying behavior:

1. **Customer Reviews:** Platforms like Amazon, Yelp, and Google have made reviews essential to buying. A study by BrightLocal found that 91% of consumers regularly or occasionally read online reviews before making a purchase. These reviews offer authenticity because they are from real people without incentives to promote a product unless they genuinely believe in it. Negative reviews, in particular, provide unique value because they highlight potential flaws consumers want to avoid. Brands must recognize that both positive and negative reviews are critical to establishing credibility. A company with only glowing reviews can actually raise suspicion among consumers.

2. **Influencers and Micro-Influencers:** Social media influencers have become powerful gatekeepers of brand trust. Influencers can sway their followers' buying decisions, from fashion to technology to home goods, with just one post. Unlike traditional celebrities, influencers build their brand on personal engagement and perceived authenticity. However, influencer marketing has also led to the rise of micro-influencers, individuals with smaller, niche followings who often have a deeper connection with their audience. These micro-influencers may not have millions of followers, but their recommendations carry significant weight within specific communities. Brands that partner with these influencers often find their messages resonate more authentically than those promoted by mainstream celebrities.

3. **User-Generated Content (UGC):** Consumers today are not just passive buyers. They actively create and share content about their experiences. This content ranges from product reviews to unboxing videos to Instagram posts showing how they use a product in their everyday lives. Brands like GoPro and Glossier have capitalized on this trend by encouraging consumers to share their stories, thus creating a cycle of authentic, unpaid advertising. This organic content is often more persuasive than traditional advertising because it feels authentic and unfiltered.

Success Stories: Brands That Understand the Modern Consumer

Several brands have successfully embraced the rise of the savvy consumer by adapting their strategies and emphasizing authenticity, transparency, and social proof.

- **Glossier:** Glossier's rise from a beauty blog to a billion-dollar brand is a testament to the power of community-building. Founder Emily Weiss leveraged her blog, *Into the Gloss*, to cultivate a loyal following of beauty enthusiasts. Instead of launching with a barrage of ads, Glossier used feedback from real women to develop its initial product line. The brand continues to engage directly with its customers, encouraging them to share their thoughts and ideas. By putting consumer voices at the heart of their product development process, Glossier has built not just a customer base but a community of advocates.
- **Warby Parker:** Another standout example is Warby Parker, the eyeglass company that disrupted the industry by offering stylish, affordable glasses online. They understood that consumers were tired of paying hundreds of dollars for eyewear and feeling like they had no alternative. Warby Parker created a business model based on affordability, transparency, and an outstanding

customer experience. Their home try-on service was revolutionary, allowing customers to test out frames in the comfort of their own homes. Warby Parker used this customer-centric approach to build trust and loyalty, ultimately reshaping how people buy eyewear.

Failure to Adapt: Lessons from Brands That Fell Behind

On the other hand, some brands failed to keep up with changes in consumer behavior. They relied too heavily on outdated strategies, misjudged the power of consumer voices, or ignored the shift toward transparency and authenticity.

- **Pepsi's Kendall Jenner Ad:** One of the most infamous marketing missteps in recent years was Pepsi's 2017 ad featuring Kendall Jenner. The ad attempted to co-opt the imagery of social justice movements but was widely criticized for trivializing serious issues like racial inequality and police brutality. The backlash on social media was immediate and severe, with consumers accusing Pepsi of being tone-deaf and opportunistic. The company quickly pulled the ad, but the damage was done. The lesson? Modern consumers demand authenticity, especially when brands engage with social or political issues. Attempts to "cash in" on causes without a genuine understanding or commitment will be met with swift rejection.
- **J.C. Penney:** Another example is J.C. Penney's misguided attempt to overhaul its pricing strategy under former CEO Ron Johnson. The department store eliminated sales and coupons, moving to an everyday low-pricing model. The problem? J.C. Penney's core customers had come to expect and enjoy the thrill of sales. By ignoring the research phase and misunderstanding their consumer base, J.C. Penney alienated its loyal shoppers. Sales plummeted, and Johnson was ousted after just 17 months.

Engaging Directly with Consumers: A Blueprint for Success

Companies must actively engage with consumers throughout the research and buying process to thrive in this new era. This means more than just responding to reviews or answering customer service calls. It requires brands to be proactive, transparent, and genuine in every interaction.

Here's how brands can build deeper connections with savvy consumers:

1. **Listen First, Act Second:** Before launching a new product or marketing campaign, brands should invest time in understanding what their customers want. This can be done through surveys, social media engagement, or simply reading and responding to online reviews. Listening to your audience allows you to develop products and messages that resonate with their needs rather than imposing your brand's vision onto them.

2. **Be Transparent About Your Weaknesses:** Modern consumers value honesty. If a product has a flaw or limitation, acknowledge it upfront. Brands that attempt to hide their shortcomings are quickly exposed in online reviews. Transparency builds trust, and trust leads to loyalty.

3. **Create Community:** Brands like Peloton and Lululemon have excelled at creating communities around their products. These communities provide a space for consumers to share their experiences, offer feedback, and feel a sense of belonging. When consumers feel like they're part of something bigger than a product purchase, they're more likely to remain loyal.

Takeaway

The rise of the savvy consumer has fundamentally altered how brands must operate. Today's buyers are informed, empowered, and skeptical. They rely on social proof, prioritize authenticity, and demand transparency at every stage of their journey. Brands that adapt to these new realities will thrive, while those that ignore them will quickly find themselves irrelevant in a marketplace that now revolves around the customer rather than the product.

Chapter 2

The Myth Of
Product-Centric Selling

On the surface, it seems straightforward: if you have a great product, people will buy it. For decades, this belief shaped marketing strategies, with brands focusing on product quality, features, and benefits to capture consumers' attention. However, consumer behavior has evolved, and so must marketing strategies. The harsh reality is that product-centric selling is no longer enough.

The Overloaded Consumer

Today's saturated marketplace overwhelms consumers with choices. Every product category is flooded with alternatives, whether in smartphones, fitness gear, or home appliances. A product that functions well, looks appealing, or is reasonably priced no longer guarantees success. Consumers seek something deeper, something that resonates with their emotions, identity, and values.

Consider the smartphone market, one of the most competitive industries worldwide. For years, companies competed by enhancing technical specifications, higher resolution, faster processors, and better cameras. Apple, however, took a different approach. Rather than focusing solely on specs, Apple emphasized design, user experience, and emotional connection. Their messaging transcended product features: "Buy an iPhone because it's an extension of who you are." This shift from product-centric to experience-centric marketing is not a trend but a necessity.

Consumers today crave emotional resonance, personal connection, and a sense of belonging.

Emotional and Psychological Drivers of Purchasing Decisions

Understanding the psychological factors behind consumer purchases is crucial for explaining why product-focused selling falls short. Buying decisions are not purely logical; they are often emotional and subconscious.

1. **Identity and Self-Expression** Consumers buy products not just for utility but because those products represent who they are. A Tesla owner, for example, isn't just purchasing an electric vehicle; they are aligning with sustainability, innovation, and progress. The car becomes a status symbol, reflecting personal values and aspirations. Brands that fail to tap into these emotional drivers by focusing solely on product features miss a crucial opportunity.

2. **Belonging and Community** Humans are inherently social, and a sense of belonging is a fundamental need. Successful brands cultivate communities where consumers feel part of something greater. Nike, for instance, has built a global community of athletes and fitness enthusiasts who rally around the brand's ethos of perseverance and achievement. It's not just about the shoes; it's about belonging to a tribe that shares your values. When consumers feel connected to a brand community, they remain loyal, even when competitors offer technically superior products.

3. **Emotional Storytelling** Storytelling is one of the most powerful tools in modern marketing. Patagonia exemplifies this with its commitment to environmental sustainability. Their

famous "Don't Buy This Jacket" campaign urged consumers to repair or reuse rather than buy new, reinforcing the company's values. This approach didn't focus on product features but on a brand story that resonated with environmentally conscious consumers, strengthening loyalty and desirability.

The Failure of Product-Centric Thinking

Many brands have faltered by prioritizing product specifications over emotional and experiential engagement. Two notable examples illustrate this:

1. **Google Glass** Google Glass, despite its cutting-edge technology and innovative features, is one of the most infamous product failures in tech history. Google focused heavily on the product's technological prowess but neglected its impact on consumers' lives, how it made them feel, and how it aligned with their self-image. The glasses were perceived as invasive, awkward, and socially unacceptable. Without a compelling emotional or cultural narrative, even revolutionary technology failed to gain traction.

2. **Jaguar's 2024 Rebranding** Jaguar's recent rebranding, replacing its iconic leaping cat logo with a minimalist wordmark, has sparked widespread criticism for diluting its brand identity. For decades, the leaping cat symbolized power, motion, and elegance, qualities synonymous with the Jaguar name. The new design, while modern and sleek, has been described as static and uninspiring, failing to evoke the exclusivity and sophistication expected of a luxury brand.

The shift to minimalism aligns with broader design trends but has drawn comparisons to generic tech logos, undermining Jaguar's distinctiveness. Public reaction has been overwhelmingly negative, with social media flooded with memes and sarcastic commentary. By abandoning a symbol deeply ingrained in its heritage, Jaguar risks alienating loyal consumers and weakening its brand's emotional resonance in the competitive luxury car market.

Understanding consumer psychology and emotional engagement is no longer optional, it is the foundation of modern branding and marketing. Brands that recognize and harness the power of identity, community, and storytelling will not only differentiate themselves but also build deeper, more meaningful relationships with their customers. In an era where consumers seek authenticity and emotional connection, businesses must go beyond selling products; they must sell experiences, values, and belonging.

From Product to Experience: Brands That Get It Right

While many brands have stumbled, others have mastered the art of combining great products with emotionally resonant experiences. These brands understand that consumers seek more than just functionality, they want connection, identity, and immersion.

1. Apple: The Power of Ecosystem and Exclusivity

Apple's success isn't just due to sleek designs or cutting-edge technology, it's rooted in the brand's ability to create an entire ecosystem of experiences around its products. From the moment customers walk into an Apple Store, they are immersed in a carefully curated environment. The minimalist store design, attentive staff, and seamless product integration all contribute to a sense of belonging to an exclusive community.

Apple's marketing strategy is also emotionally driven. Instead of focusing solely on technical specifications, the brand sells a lifestyle. Campaigns like "Think Different" didn't promote computers; they promoted creativity, individuality, and innovation. This emotional appeal transforms customers into loyal advocates who buy into Apple's philosophy as much as its products.

2. Peloton: Building Community Through Experience

Peloton didn't revolutionize fitness simply by making a high-quality stationary bike, it created an entire fitness ecosystem that fosters motivation, engagement, and community. Through live and on-demand interactive classes, social features, and performance tracking, Peloton brings the energy of a group workout into individual homes. The brand taps into deeper emotional needs like personal growth, social connection, and accountability.

Peloton's success illustrates how companies can transform a standard product into an engaging experience. Consumers aren't just buying a bike; they're investing in a lifestyle, a support system, and a sense of achievement. However, poor financial management has challenged its long-term sustainability, showing that even strong experiential brands must ensure operational efficiency.

Why Experiences Matter More Than Products

To succeed in today's marketplace, brands must go beyond selling products and start crafting memorable, emotionally resonant experiences. Experiences that align with consumers' identities are far more valuable than product features alone.

1. Emotion Drives Decision-Making

Research shows that emotions influence up to 95% of purchasing decisions. Consumers are more likely to choose a brand based on how it makes them feel rather than its technical advantages. This emotional connection explains why luxury brands like Louis Vuitton or Rolex can command premium pricing. The allure isn't just about superior craftsmanship, it's about the exclusivity, success, and status that owning these products conveys.

2. Experiences Build Loyalty

A well-made product may earn a one-time purchase, but a powerful experience fosters long-term loyalty. Brands that prioritize superior customer experiences, whether through personalized recommendations, exceptional service, or immersive engagement, build deep emotional bonds with their consumers. These bonds often outweigh competitive pricing or incremental product improvements, ensuring sustained customer retention.

Takeaway

The rise of the experience economy has dismantled the traditional product-centric selling model. In today's competitive landscape, having a great product is no longer enough. Consumers expect brands to offer more, they crave emotional engagement, personal connection, and a sense of belonging. Companies that fail to move beyond features and benefits will struggle to stay relevant. The brands that thrive will be those that recognize that purchasing decisions are driven by the heart as much as the mind.

Chapter 3

Building Brands
Vs. Selling Products

In modern commerce, there is a critical distinction between selling products and building a brand. A product is tangible, it fulfills a need or solves a problem. A brand, however, is intangible; it represents the emotional and psychological relationship between a company and its customers. The difference between these two approaches often separates companies that achieve short-term success from those that cultivate enduring customer loyalty.

The Power of Brand Identity

Consider this example: Two companies sell nearly identical water bottles. Both are well-designed, eco-friendly, and reasonably priced. However, Company A markets its bottle based on technical specifications, leakproof design, BPA-free materials, and superior insulation. Company B takes a different approach. Instead of just selling a product, it builds a narrative around the bottle: it symbolizes sustainability, adventure, and mindfulness. The company partners with environmental organizations, uses social media to share stories of outdoor enthusiasts, and emphasizes its mission to reduce single-use plastic waste.

Over time, Company B's customers aren't just buying a water bottle; they're buying into a lifestyle. They feel part of a movement. Even though the bottles from both companies are nearly identical in quality,

Company B's bottle becomes far more desirable because it's tied to something bigger, identity and purpose.

This example illustrates the difference between selling a product and building a brand. Products solve problems, but brands create connections. A great product might attract consumers, but a strong brand keeps them coming back. Modern consumers crave connection. While products focused on technical specifications face constant competition, brands establish deeper relationships that are harder to break.

The Anatomy of a Strong Brand

What makes a strong brand, and why do consumers gravitate toward it?

1. **Consistency Across Touchpoints**: A brand isn't just a logo or a tagline, it's the sum of every interaction a consumer has with a company, from websites and social media to customer service. Successful brands ensure that every touchpoint aligns with their core values. Starbucks, for example, isn't just selling coffee, it's selling an experience. Whether in New York, Tokyo, or Paris, the ambiance, service, and even the barista's language remain consistent, reinforcing trust and brand identity.

2. **A Clear Mission and Values**: Today's consumers are more values-driven. They want to know what a brand stands for, not just what it sells. Companies that clearly articulate and stick to a mission build stronger loyalty. Take Patagonia, for instance. The outdoor clothing company has made environmental activism a core part of its identity, not just through messaging, but through tangible actions, like donating profits to environmental causes and encouraging customers to repair old gear instead of buying new products. By aligning its mission with its offerings, Patagonia has built a brand that customers trust and admire.

3. **Emotional Resonance**: People don't just buy products, they buy feelings. Whether it's the sense of accomplishment from wearing Nike, the security of owning a Volvo, or the luxury of

carrying a Louis Vuitton bag, consumers are drawn to brands that evoke emotions. Emotional resonance goes beyond features and benefits; it taps into deeper psychological needs like safety, status, and self-expression.

Case Study: Apple – Mastering the Art of Brand Building

One of the most iconic examples of successful brand-building is Apple. While Apple products are innovative and well-designed, it's the brand that sets the company apart.

Apple's messaging has always been about simplicity, creativity, and challenging the status quo. From its early "Think Different" campaign to its modern-day marketing, Apple has consistently positioned itself as the brand for innovators, creators, and forward-thinkers. It's not just selling computers or phones, it's empowering people to express themselves through technology.

By emphasizing these core values, Apple has cultivated one of the world's most loyal customer bases. Customers aren't just buying products; they're buying into a community of like-minded individuals who value innovation and design. Even when competitors offer products with similar or superior specifications, many consumers remain fiercely loyal to Apple because of the emotional connection they've built over time.

Apple's retail stores also extend this brand identity. They're designed not just as places to buy products but as immersive experiences, minimalist spaces where customers interact with products, receive personal support, and feel like part of the Apple ecosystem. Every aspect of Apple's brand is carefully curated to reinforce its identity and values.

The Shortcomings of Product-Centric Companies

While brands like Apple, Nike, and Patagonia have succeeded by focusing on brand-building, others have struggled due to a product-centric mindset. A notable example is GoPro.

At its peak, GoPro dominated the action camera market, offering high-quality, durable cameras. But GoPro made a critical mistake, it focused too much on its product and not enough on brand identity. While its early marketing relied heavily on user-generated content, it failed to evolve beyond the product. When competitors introduced similar or better cameras, GoPro struggled to differentiate itself. Its marketing continued emphasizing technical specs rather than building a deeper emotional connection with its audience. As a result, GoPro became just another camera company rather than a lasting brand.

Another example is Sonos, which built a great brand but nearly destroyed it through poor execution. In May 2024, Sonos released a major update to its mobile app, aiming to enhance user experience and accelerate innovation. However, the rollout was riddled with issues: customers encountered numerous bugs, lost access to basic features like playlist editing and alarms, and, in some cases, couldn't access their entire music libraries. This led to widespread dissatisfaction and significant financial repercussions.

Adding to the problem, Sonos failed to publicly address the crisis until July. Loyal customers felt abandoned. The company lost $53 million in one quarter, and CEO Patrick Spence ultimately lost his job.

In response, Sonos committed to more rigorous pre-launch testing, gradual rollouts of major changes, and the establishment of a customer advisory board. Additionally, Sonos extended warranties for its home speaker products and announced that its executive team would forgo bonuses unless product improvements were made. However, at the time of writing, the damage to customer trust remained unresolved.

The Long-Term Benefits of Brand Building

Brand-building isn't just about making an immediate sale, it's about creating lasting value. Companies that prioritize strong brand identity and emotional connection enjoy several advantages:

1. **Loyalty in a Crowded Market**: When consumers feel connected to a brand, they're less likely to switch to competitors. For example, despite competition in the fitness industry, Peloton has cultivated a fiercely loyal following by positioning itself around community and lifestyle.
2. **Pricing Power**: A strong brand enables companies to charge a premium. Consumers often pay more for a product from a brand they trust and admire. Luxury brands like Chanel, Tesla, and Gucci thrive on brand equity, allowing them to maintain high price points while retaining market share.
3. **Cultural Influence**: Successful brands shape culture. Nike's "Just Do It" slogan, for instance, has transcended sports and entered everyday language. Brands with cultural influence maintain longevity, even in volatile markets.

The Future of Branding: Purpose-Driven Companies

As branding evolves, consumers increasingly favor purpose-driven companies, businesses that stand for something beyond profit. Millennials and Gen Z prioritize brands that align with their values, such as sustainability, diversity, and social responsibility. Companies that embrace these causes authentically will build long-term relationships with customers.

For example, Ben & Jerry's has fully embraced its role as a socially conscious brand. From climate activism to racial justice advocacy, the company ties its identity to progressive values. This approach strengthens customer loyalty, as consumers willingly pay more for products from brands they believe in.

Takeaway

In today's competitive landscape, building a strong brand is far more valuable than simply selling a product. Brands that focus on emotional resonance, consistency, and authenticity create lasting customer relationships, driving long-term loyalty and success. Companies that invest in brand-building won't just survive, they'll thrive in a world where identity, values, and connection matter more than ever.

Chapter 4

Authenticity:
The New Currency
Of Consumer Trust

In a world overwhelmed by advertising, marketing messages, and influencer endorsements, consumers have developed a refined ability to distinguish between brands that are genuine and those that are not.

Authenticity has become the new standard by which modern consumers judge the companies they choose to support. More than flashy ads or celebrity endorsements, today's buyers crave honesty, transparency, and alignment with their values.

At the heart of consumer decision-making today lies a simple truth: no matter how exceptional a product is, how big a marketing budget is, or how many influencers a brand enlists, authenticity is non-negotiable. Consumers can quickly spot inauthenticity, and once a brand is perceived as insincere, it risks losing trust and loyalty, often for good.

Everlane, once celebrated for its "radical transparency" ethos, faced significant scrutiny in early 2020 when employees and former employees spoke out against the company's purportedly progressive values. Accusations included union-busting tactics after several customer service workers organizing a union were let go, as well as a broader disconnect between Everlane's public-facing image and its internal culture, particularly concerning diversity, equity, and inclusion. These revelations clashed with the brand's heavily promoted commitment to ethical practices and transparent supply chains, casting doubt on Everlane's authenticity. Many consumers, who had championed Everlane for its socially conscious stance, felt misled by the incongruence between its marketing and reported behavior, resulting in widespread criticism across social media and news outlets.

This backlash had notable repercussions for Everlane's reputation and bottom line. Once a hallmark of the brand, customer trust eroded as calls for boycotts spread online. The timing of the company's employee layoffs during the pandemic only heightened concerns about union-busting and management practices. As a result, Everlane experienced declines in sales growth compared to prior years, with some longtime supporters opting to purchase from competitor brands they perceived as more genuinely mission-driven. While Everlane has continued to operate and address some of the concerns, such as announcing new diversity and inclusion initiatives, the controversy remains a cautionary tale about how quickly a values-based brand's credibility can suffer when internal realities conflict with external messaging.

The Rise of the Authentic Consumer Authenticity is more than just a buzzword; it's a fundamental shift in how consumers interact with brands. Millennials and Gen Z, in particular, are driving this change. These younger generations, having grown up with the internet and social media, are highly attuned to marketing tactics and quick to call out companies that don't live up to their promises.

But why is authenticity so important to them?

1. **Mistrust of Traditional Advertising:** Decades of being bombarded by manipulative and exaggerated advertisements have made consumers more skeptical than ever before. Old-school marketing tactics, where brands made grand promises that rarely aligned with the reality of their products, have eroded consumer trust. Today's consumers know when they are "being

sold to" and don't like it. They prefer brands that are upfront about what they stand for and who they are.

2. **Desire for Meaningful Connections:** Modern consumers want to feel connected to the brands they support. They want to know that a brand's values align with their own and that their purchases contribute to something meaningful. Authenticity is vital to building these connections. Brands that foster a sense of belonging, shared values, and genuine engagement are the ones that consumers return to time and time again.

3. **Transparency in the Digital Age:** In the age of social media and instant information, brands have nowhere to hide. If a company is insincere in its messaging or tries to cover up mistakes, it will inevitably be exposed. This transparency demands that brands always operate with integrity, both in public and behind closed doors.

Let's look at some brands that have built their success on authenticity and how they have connected deeply with consumers.

Case Study: TOMS – Building a Brand on Purpose

One of the most well-known examples of authenticity in action is TOMS, the footwear company that built its brand on the promise of giving back. TOMS' One for One model, in which the company donated a pair of shoes for every pair purchased, resonated deeply with socially conscious consumers.

From the outset, TOMS was authentic in its mission. The company didn't just talk about doing good; it embedded the concept into the core of its business model. Every purchase had a tangible impact, and consumers felt good about contributing to a cause that mattered. This transparency and alignment of values made TOMS a household name among Millennials, who prioritize ethical and socially responsible purchases.

TOMS' authenticity extended beyond just marketing. It was part of their identity. The founder, Blake Mycoskie, became the face of the brand, sharing his personal story of why he started the company and how his travels inspired the One for One model in Argentina, where he saw children in need of shoes. TOMS successfully built an emotional connection with its customers by focusing on a clear, genuine purpose.

TOMS footwear is currently facing challenges, struggling to regain its popularity and market share, mainly due to a shift away from its "one-for-one" business model and difficulty adapting to changing fashion trends. However, the company is attempting to rebrand and reposition itself to attract new customers while maintaining its core values by donating a portion of its profits to charitable causes.

Case Study: Warby Parker – Authenticity Through Accessibility

Another brand that has successfully built authenticity into its identity is Warby Parker. This eyewear company disrupted the industry by offering stylish, affordable glasses online. Warby Parker's authenticity comes from its mission to make eyewear more accessible to everyone without sacrificing style or quality.

From the beginning, Warby Parker was upfront about its goals: to offer high-quality glasses at a fraction of the cost of traditional retailers. They also implemented a Buy a Pair, Give a Pair program, donating glasses to people in need for every pair sold. Like TOMS, this socially conscious model resonated with customers who wanted to feel like their purchases made a positive impact.

However, what truly set Warby Parker apart was its transparency. They explained why glasses were so expensive with a few large companies controlling the market, and they were upfront about how they could sell theirs for less by cutting out the middleman. This level of honesty made customers feel like they were making an informed, empowered decision when they chose Warby Parker over traditional retailers. By demystifying the process and openly sharing their business practices, Warby Parker built trust with their audience and, as a result, built loyalty.

The Dangers of Faking Authenticity

For every brand that has succeeded through authenticity, an equal number have failed by attempting to fake it. In the age of transparency, inauthenticity is not only exposed but also punished. Consumers have little patience for companies that pretend to care about social causes or adopt a "woke" stance purely for marketing.

Let's examine two infamous examples of brands that tried to fake authenticity and faced significant backlash.

Pepsi's Kendall Jenner Ad

In 2017, Pepsi aired an ad featuring Kendall Jenner, in which she seemingly brings peace to a protest by handing a police officer a Pepsi. The ad was intended to tap into the energy of social justice movements, but instead, it came off as tone-deaf and exploitative. Pepsi's attempt to co-opt the imagery of real struggles for racial equality and police reform backfired spectacularly. Consumers saw through the marketing ploy and criticized the company for trivializing serious issues to sell soda. The backlash was swift and severe, forcing Pepsi to pull the ad and issue an apology. This incident highlighted the dangers of adopting a cause without fully understanding or committing to it.

H&M's "Conscious" Collection

Another example is H&M, which launched a "Conscious" collection of clothing made from sustainable materials. While the campaign appeared to align with growing consumer demand for eco-friendly products, the company was criticized for greenwashing, falsely presenting itself as environmentally friendly while continuing fast fashion practices that contribute to environmental degradation. The public quickly called out the disconnect between H&M's messaging and its actual business model, accusing the brand of using sustainability as a marketing tool rather than demonstrating a genuine commitment. The backlash damaged H&M's

reputation, proving that consumers will not tolerate brands that try to fake authenticity.

How Brands Can Embed Authenticity Into Their DNA

Authenticity cannot be manufactured or added as an afterthought. It must be embedded in the very core of a brand, integrated into the company's mission, values, and treatment of customers, employees, and the environment. Here are some key strategies brands can use to foster genuine authenticity:

1. **Align Actions with Words** – Authentic brands don't just talk about their values, they live them. If a company claims to care about sustainability, it should back that up with tangible actions, such as reducing its carbon footprint, using sustainable materials, or donating to environmental causes. Consumers can spot inauthenticity from a mile away, so brands must ensure their actions reflect their messaging.

2. **Be Transparent About Mistakes** – No brand is perfect, and consumers don't expect them to be. What they do expect is honesty. When mistakes happen, and they will, authentic brands own up to them. Whether it's a faulty product, a misguided campaign, or a corporate scandal, how a company handles its missteps can make all the difference. Apologizing, taking responsibility, and outlining clear steps to address the issue builds trust and shows consumers that the brand is committed to doing better.

3. **Engage with Customers** – Authenticity thrives on two-way communication. Brands that listen to their customers and engage in meaningful dialogue are more likely to build genuine relationships. This means responding to both positive and negative feedback and taking consumer input seriously. Brands like Glossier and Airbnb excel by creating platforms where

customers can share their experiences, ask questions, and contribute to the conversation.

4. **Stay True to Core Values** – In the pursuit of growth and market share, it can be tempting for brands to stray from their original values. However, staying true to those core principles is crucial for maintaining authenticity. This doesn't mean brands can't evolve; every company must adapt to changing times. However, their evolution should be guided by the values that made them successful in the first place.

The Role of Corporate Social Responsibility (CSR)

Corporate social responsibility (CSR) has become increasingly important in consumers' purchasing decisions. Brands that engage in CSR through charitable giving, sustainable practices, or ethical labor standards are seen as more trustworthy and authentic. However, it's not enough to adopt CSR initiatives purely for marketing purposes. Consumers can tell when a company's efforts are genuine and when it's just checking boxes to appear responsible.

Brands that succeed in this area integrate CSR into their core business model rather than treating it as an add-on. For example, The Body Shop has long been a leader in ethical beauty, championing fair trade and animal cruelty-free products since its inception. The brand's commitment to these causes is evident in every aspect of its business, from sourcing ingredients to advocating for animal rights. Because CSR is central to The Body Shop's identity, consumers trust that the brand's efforts are authentic.

Takeaway

In today's marketplace, authenticity is everything. Consumers want to support brands that are transparent, honest, and aligned with their values. Brands that build authenticity into their DNA are rewarded with trust, loyalty, and long-term success. On the other hand, those that attempt to fake authenticity or adopt social causes purely for marketing risk losing their credibility, and, in turn, their customers. Authenticity isn't just a strategy; it's a necessity in a world where trust is the ultimate currency.

Chapter 5

The Power Of Social Media And Influencers

Once upon a time, advertising was a one-way conversation. Brands projected their messages through television, radio, or print, and consumers passively received them. Those days are long gone.

Today, the relationship between brands and consumers is far more dynamic, thanks to social media. Platforms like Instagram, TikTok, Twitter, and YouTube have created an interactive space where brands and consumers communicate directly and in real time. This environment allows brands to build trust, share stories, and, most importantly, leverage influencers to shape consumer perceptions and drive sales.

The Rise of Social Media: Where Conversations Happen

Social media has become the beating heart of brand-consumer relationships. With billions of active users across various platforms, it's where people discover new products, share opinions, and engage with companies in ways that were unimaginable just a decade ago.

For brands, social media is not just a place to advertise, it's a place to engage, listen, and build relationships. Unlike traditional advertising, which relies on broad messaging, social media allows for personalized, targeted interactions. Brands can connect directly with customers, answer questions, respond to feedback, and resolve customer service issues in real time.

Why Social Media is Critical to Brand Success

1. **Accessibility and Visibility** – Social media provides unparalleled access to consumers. A well-crafted Instagram post or tweet can reach millions in seconds. It also enables brands to engage with customers globally, breaking geographical barriers.
2. **Building Communities** – Social media allows brands to create loyal communities. Companies like Peloton and Glossier have succeeded not just by selling products but by fostering spaces where customers feel heard, supported, and connected. Through Facebook groups, Instagram hashtags, and TikTok challenges, brands can cultivate organic word-of-mouth marketing.
3. **Real-Time Feedback** – One of social media's greatest advantages is instant consumer feedback. Comments, likes, and shares provide brands with invaluable insights to guide product development and marketing strategies.

The Power of Influencers: Modern-Day Opinion Leaders

Perhaps the most impactful development in social media marketing has been the rise of influencers, content creators who build large followings and sway audience opinions and purchasing decisions. But what makes influencers so effective, and why are they a crucial part of modern marketing?

Influencers are powerful because they are perceived as trusted sources. Their followers view them as more authentic and relatable than traditional celebrities or corporate marketing. By sharing their personal lives, struggles, and successes, influencers create a level of intimacy that most brands struggle to achieve independently.

However, not all influencers are created equal. They range from mega-influencers with millions of followers to nano-influencers with just a few thousand but highly engaged audiences. Brands must carefully select the right type of influencer based on their goals.

Types of Influencers and Their Impact

1. **Mega-Influencers** – Social media celebrities like Kylie Jenner and Cristiano Ronaldo boast tens of millions of followers. Their endorsements offer massive reach but often come with a hefty price tag and can sometimes feel more like traditional advertising than genuine recommendations.
2. **Macro-Influencers** – With 100,000 to a million followers, macro-influencers are often niche celebrities, such as fitness gurus or tech reviewers. They provide significant reach while maintaining a strong connection to their audience.
3. **Micro-Influencers** – These influencers, with 10,000 to 100,000 followers, have highly engaged audiences. Their recommendations carry more weight due to their perceived authenticity and close-knit community relationships. Brands targeting specific demographics benefit significantly from micro-influencers.
4. **Nano-Influencers** – With fewer than 10,000 followers, nano-influencers operate within niche or local communities. Their deep connections with followers create highly trusted endorsements, making them ideal for grassroots marketing efforts.

Successful Influencer Marketing: Case Studies

The power of influencers is best illustrated through brands that have effectively leveraged them to build trust and drive sales. Here are two standout examples:

Glossier: Building a Brand Through Community

Glossier, the beauty brand, built its business around social media and influencer marketing rather than traditional advertising. The company relied on influencers, ranging from everyday users to beauty bloggers, to generate buzz around its products. By sending products for review and encouraging influencers to share personal experiences, Glossier created a sense of authenticity and trust. The brand also engaged directly with customers on Instagram, promoting user-generated content and featuring real customers in its marketing. This grassroots approach helped disrupt the beauty industry and build a loyal following.

Gymshark: Fitness Influencers Driving Growth

Gymshark, a fitness apparel brand, successfully leveraged influencers to grow its business. The company partnered with fitness influencers on Instagram and YouTube to showcase real people using its gear during workouts. This strategy resonated with the fitness community, creating an authentic connection between the brand and its audience. Gymshark's influencers didn't just promote the brand; they embodied its lifestyle, fueling strong customer loyalty and rapid growth.

Authenticity in Influencer Marketing: What Works and What Doesn't

As influencer marketing continues to grow, one key factor remains critical: authenticity. Consumers are highly attuned to authenticity on social media and can quickly discern when an influencer is promoting a product solely for financial gain. Brands that misuse influencer marketing by partnering with influencers who lack a genuine connection to the product risk alienating their audience and damaging their credibility.

For influencer marketing to be effective, the partnership must feel natural and authentic. Influencers should only promote products they genuinely believe in, and the content should align with their usual tone and style. When done right, influencer marketing feels like a trusted recommendation from a friend. However, when executed poorly, it can come across as a hollow advertisement, turning consumers away from both the influencer and the brand.

Missteps in Influencer Marketing

While there have been many success stories in influencer marketing, there have also been notable failures. These missteps often stem from a lack of alignment between the brand and the influencer, as well as inadequate disclosure of sponsorships, which can erode trust.

1. **Fyre Festival: A Case Study in Deception**
   One of the most infamous influencer marketing disasters was the Fyre Festival. Promoted as an ultra-luxury music festival in the Bahamas, Fyre Festival used influencers like Kendall Jenner, Bella Hadid, and other high-profile models to promote the event on Instagram. The influencers posted glamorous images of a paradise getaway, leading thousands of people to purchase expensive tickets. However, the reality was far from what was promised, attendees arrived to find a disaster zone with no accommodations, food, or organization. The festival became a cautionary tale about the dangers of false advertising and the risks of influencers endorsing products they know little about. Many influencers faced backlash for misleading their followers, proving the importance of genuine and informed endorsements.

2. **Kim Kardashian's Misaligned Product Endorsements**
   Kim Kardashian, a mega-influencer, has faced criticism for promoting products that don't align with her image or values. For example, her endorsement of appetite-suppressing lollipops clashed with her role as a body-positive influencer and role model for women. These endorsements led to backlash from her followers and the broader public, accusing her of promoting unhealthy ideals for financial gain. This serves as a reminder that even the most influential figures can lose credibility if their endorsements feel disingenuous or exploitative.

Engagement Beyond Influencers: How Brands Can Succeed on Social Media

While influencers are a powerful tool, they are only part of a broader social media strategy. To build genuine engagement, brands must go beyond influencer partnerships and actively interact with their audience. Here's how brands can succeed on social media:

1. **Tell Your Story**
   Consumers want to connect with brands on a personal level. Share your brand's origins, mission, and values. Use platforms like Instagram and YouTube to give customers a behind-the-scenes look at your company, your products, and your people.

2. **Engage in Two-Way Conversations**
   Social media is not just a platform for broadcasting messages, it's an opportunity for dialogue. Respond to comments, answer questions, and participate in conversations to foster a sense of community and trust.

3. **Leverage User-Generated Content**
   Encourage customers to create content featuring your products. Whether through a branded hashtag or a product challenge, user-generated content adds authenticity and social proof. Featuring real customers using your product can be more impactful than any paid advertisement.

4. **Maintain Consistency Across Platforms**
   A cohesive brand identity is essential. Ensure that your brand's voice, visuals, and messaging remain consistent across Instagram, TikTok, Twitter, and Facebook. Consistency builds recognition and strengthens brand loyalty.

The power of social media and influencers cannot be overstated in today's consumer landscape. Social platforms provide brands with an opportunity to connect with consumers on a personal level, while influencers offer the trust and authenticity that modern buyers crave. However, success in this space requires more than simply leveraging influencers, it demands genuine engagement, strategic partnerships, and a commitment to maintaining authenticity in every interaction.

Brands that master the art of social media and influencer marketing will thrive in this new era of consumer trust. By building authentic communities and fostering meaningful relationships, they can achieve lasting success beyond a single transaction.

Truff's rapid rise to success can be largely attributed to its strategic use of social media, which played a crucial role in building brand awareness, credibility, and sales.

From the beginning, Truff recognized that standing out in the crowded hot sauce market required a visually compelling brand that would thrive on social media, particularly Instagram. They invested in high-quality, aesthetic product photography, featuring sleek packaging, a distinctive geometric bottle cap, and a consistent, premium color scheme. By positioning its brand as a luxury lifestyle product rather than just another condiment, Truff became highly shareable and visually appealing to its target audience.

Instagram became Truff's primary marketing channel, where they curated a food-forward, high-end aesthetic that reinforced their premium status. They leveraged short-form videos, engaging stories, and direct interactions with followers to build a sense of community. Before officially launching, they teased the product with mysterious preview campaigns, creating curiosity and demand. This early focus on brand-building rather than just product-selling set them apart from competitors.

One of the biggest drivers of Truff's early growth was influencer marketing. Instead of relying on traditional advertising, they strategically partnered with micro-influencers, food bloggers, and lifestyle personalities with engaged followings. These influencers received free products in exchange for organic, high-quality content featuring Truff. As word spread, more prominent influencers and celebrities took notice, leading to high-profile endorsements from figures like the Kardashians and Drake. Additionally, being featured on the popular YouTube show "Hot Ones" gave Truff credibility and exposure to a massive audience. These influencer collaborations helped expand their reach beyond traditional hot sauce consumers, positioning the brand as a must-have culinary item for foodies and luxury shoppers.

Truff also leveraged user-generated content (UGC) to expand its reach further. They encouraged customers to share photos, videos, and recipes using Truff, which they then reshared on their social media channels. Branded hashtags like #Truff helped fans easily tag and connect with the brand. To strengthen customer engagement, they frequently interacted with followers, responded to comments and direct messages, and ran giveaways to encourage more content creation. This community-driven approach turned Truff customers into brand ambassadors, providing them with free word-of-mouth marketing at scale.

Once they had established a strong organic presence, Truff amplified their success with paid social media advertising. They ran highly targeted Instagram and Facebook ads, focusing on retargeting users who had visited their website or engaged with their content. These ads included high-quality visuals, influencer testimonials, and short-form videos, which blended seamlessly into users' feeds, making them feel less like traditional advertisements and more like recommendations. By using data-driven insights to optimize their campaigns, Truff ensured that their advertising spend was efficient, leading to rapid sales growth.

Scarcity and exclusivity also played a role in Truff's viral success. They created limited-edition products, such as their White Truffle Hot Sauce, generating urgency and excitement among their audience. Truff often teased new launches exclusively on Instagram, building hype and anticipation before products were available. They also established a

> *pre-launch waitlist for their retail expansion, making customers feel like*
> *they were part of an exclusive club. This FOMO (fear of missing out)*
> *strategy drove engagement and sales, reinforcing their status as a*
> *premium brand.*
>
> *By combining stunning branding, strategic influencer partnerships, user-*
> *generated content, targeted ads, and scarcity tactics, Truff built a massive*
> *social media presence before even entering major retail stores. Their efforts*
> *led to celebrity endorsements, viral brand awareness, and millions in*
> *sales, all driven by their ability to turn their hot sauce into a luxury*
> *lifestyle product. Their success is a testament to the power of leveraging*
> *social media correctly, not just to sell but to create an aspirational brand*
> *that people want to be a part of.*
>
> *For brands looking to replicate Truff's strategy, the key is to prioritize*
> *high-quality content, engage with your audience authentically, partner*
> *with the right influencers, and create an experience that extends beyond*
> *the product itself. By doing so, brands can cultivate a loyal following,*
> *generate organic buzz, and drive explosive growth.*

Each social media platform serves a unique purpose and reaches different audiences. Here's how you can use them effectively to communicate with prospective customers for your business:

1. Facebook

- **Audience**: Broad demographic, slightly older (25-55+).
- **Best for**: Brand awareness, community building, paid advertising.
- **How to use it**:
  - Create a business page with engaging visuals and regular posts.
  - Use Facebook Groups to build a community around your brand.
  - Run targeted ads to reach specific customer segments.

o Use Facebook Live to highlight products, share insights, or host Q&A sessions.

2. Instagram

- **Audience**: Younger audience (18-45), visual.
- **Best for**: Brand aesthetics, influencer marketing, direct sales.
- **How to use it**:
  o Post high-quality images and videos of your products.
  o Use Instagram Stories & Reels to provide quick, engaging content.
  o Leverage influencers or brand ambassadors to reach a wider audience.
  o Utilize Instagram Shopping to allow customers to make direct purchases.

3. LinkedIn

- **Audience**: Professionals, B2B businesses, and decision-makers.
- **Best for**: Thought leadership, networking, and B2B sales.
- **How to use it**:
  o Share industry insights, case studies, and success stories.
  o Publish articles and engage in professional discussions.
  o Connect with potential business partners and customers.
  o Use LinkedIn Ads to target professionals based on job titles and industries.

4. Twitter (X)

- **Audience**: News-oriented, professionals, younger audience.
- **Best for**: Customer service, trending topics, real-time updates.
- **How to use it**:
  o Engage in conversations around industry trends and hashtags.
  o Provide quick customer support and answer inquiries.

- o Share business updates, promotions, and links to new content.
- o Use Twitter Ads to increase reach and engagement.

5. TikTok

- **Audience**: Younger audience (13-35), creative and trend-driven.
- **Best for**: Short-form video marketing, viral challenges, and brand storytelling.
- **How to use it**:
  - o Create fun, engaging, and educational videos about your brand or products.
  - o Participate in trends and challenges to gain visibility.
  - o Collaborate with TikTok influencers to tap into their audience.
  - o Use TikTok Ads to reach a highly engaged user base.

6. Pinterest

- **Audience**: Primarily female, DIY enthusiasts, and shoppers.
- **Best for**: Visual inspiration, eCommerce, product discovery.
- **How to use it**:
  - o Pin high-quality images and infographics with links to your website.
  - o Create themed boards to display product categories.
  - o Use rich pins to add more product details.
  - o Run Pinterest Ads to drive website traffic and sales.

7. YouTube

- **Audience**: All demographics, high engagement with video content.
- **Best for**: Educational content, long-form storytelling, and product demonstrations.
- **How to use it**:

- o Create how-to videos, tutorials, and product reviews.
- o Use YouTube Shorts for quick, engaging content.
- o Optimize video titles and descriptions for searchability.
- o Run video ads targeting specific audience segments.

8. Reddit

- **Audience**: Niche communities, engaged users, high skepticism towards ads.
- **Best for**: Thought leadership, customer engagement, market research.
- **How to use it**:
  - o Participate in relevant subreddits with value-driven content.
  - o Answer questions and provide insights without being overly promotional.
  - o Run Reddit Ads targeted at specific communities.
  - o Host AMAs (Ask Me Anything) to connect with your audience.

9. Snapchat

- **Audience**: Young users (13-30), casual and personal communication.
- **Best for**: Short-lived promotions, brand personality, user engagement.
- **How to use it**:
  - o Create behind-the-scenes content to display your brand.
  - o Use Snapchat Stories and filters for promotions.
  - o Engage with younger customers through exclusive deals.
  - o Use Snapchat Ads to reach mobile-focused users.

10. WhatsApp & Messenger

- **Audience**: All demographics, direct customer communication.
- **Best for**: Customer service, personalized communication, direct sales.

- **How to use it:**

  o Use WhatsApp Business for automated responses and catalog features.

  o Offer customer support and resolve inquiries quickly.

  o Use broadcast lists for promotions and updates.

  o Integrate with Facebook Messenger Ads for direct engagement.

Takeaway

- **B2C Businesses** should focus on Instagram, Facebook, TikTok, YouTube, and Pinterest for visual marketing.

- **B2B Businesses** should leverage LinkedIn, Twitter, and YouTube for networking and expertise.

- **Customer Service** works best on Twitter, WhatsApp, and Messenger.

- **SEO & Content-Driven Brands** should use YouTube, Reddit, and Pinterest for long-term discoverability.

Chapter 6

The Customer Journey: From Discovery To Loyalty

It takes approximately 7.5 hours of content consumption for a prospective customer to build enough trust in a brand to make a meaningful buying decision.

Modern consumerism is no longer a straightforward path from product awareness to purchase. Instead, the customer journey has evolved into a complex series of touchpoints that influence how, when, and why a customer buys. To succeed in today's market, brands must recognize that every interaction, whether an ad, a customer review, or a post-purchase experience, shapes consumer perception and loyalty.

The key to success lies in understanding the different stages of the customer journey and leveraging each stage to build deeper relationships. Brands that master this journey, from Discovery to Loyalty, can create seamless, personalized experiences that foster long-term customer engagement and retention.

The Four Stages of the Customer Journey

The modern customer journey is typically divided into four key stages:

1. **Awareness**, when a consumer first becomes aware of your brand.

2. **Consideration**, when a consumer evaluates your product against competitors.
3. **Purchase**, when a consumer decides to buy.
4. **Loyalty**, when a consumer becomes a repeat customer and brand advocate.

Each stage presents unique opportunities for engagement. Brands that optimize each touchpoint can effectively move consumers from discovery to loyalty, enhancing their overall customer experience.

Stage 1: Awareness , The First Point of Contact

The Awareness stage is where customers first learn about your brand or product. This could happen through various channels, such as an Instagram ad, a blog post, a YouTube video, or even word-of-mouth. In today's crowded marketplace, cutting through the noise and capturing consumer attention is more challenging than ever.

However, awareness isn't just about making a first impression, it's about making the right impression. Your brand must be memorable and relevant from the first interaction. Consumers are bombarded with ads and content daily, so your brand needs to stand out both visually and in terms of messaging and value.

You can be better, or you can be different. Ideally, you should be both. But you can't stand out if you can't answer the question: *What makes your brand different from your competitors?*

Creating Effective Awareness

1. **Targeted Advertising**: Digital advertising on platforms like Facebook, Instagram, and Google enables brands to reach specific demographics based on interests, behaviors, and online activity. Instead of casting a wide net, focusing on a targeted audience ensures that your brand reaches consumers most likely to be interested in your offering.

2. **Content Marketing**: Providing valuable content is another powerful way to build awareness. Blog posts, infographics, and educational videos can establish your brand as an authority in your field. Companies like HubSpot excel at this by offering free, insightful content that helps their audience while subtly introducing their services.

3. **Influencer Marketing**: Partnering with influencers can effectively generate awareness. Influencers introduce your product to their followers in a relatable and authentic way, often giving you access to new audiences that traditional advertising might not reach.

Example: Airbnb

In its early days, Airbnb faced the challenge of raising awareness about an entirely new concept, staying in someone's home instead of a hotel. They invested heavily in visually engaging social media ads and promoted real stories of travelers having unique experiences. Rather than focusing solely on the practical aspects of their service, Airbnb tapped into the emotions and adventure-seeking nature of their target audience. This storytelling approach made Airbnb memorable and piqued curiosity, pushing potential customers into the Consideration phase.

Stage 2: Consideration , The Research Phase

Once consumers become aware of your brand, they enter the Consideration phase. Here, potential customers research and evaluate their options. Today's consumers are more empowered than ever to conduct thorough research before making a purchase. They compare prices, read reviews, watch unboxing videos, and consult friends or influencers for opinions.

Brands that excel in this phase provide helpful resources, build trust, and clearly differentiate themselves from competitors. Consumers in this stage seek answers to questions such as:

- How does this product solve my problem?
- What makes it better than other options?
- Can I trust this brand?

Engaging Consumers in the Consideration Phase

1. **Customer Reviews and Testimonials**: Social proof is a powerful influencer in purchasing decisions. Platforms like Amazon and Yelp have shown how crucial customer reviews are in shaping consumer trust. Brands should actively encourage customer reviews and engage with them by responding to both positive and negative feedback to demonstrate attentiveness and transparency.

2. **Educational Content**: Brands can use blog posts, videos, and case studies to help consumers make informed decisions. For instance, Backcountry, an online outdoor gear retailer, provides in-depth guides on choosing the right gear for different activities. These guides don't just promote products; they educate the consumer, building trust and credibility during the decision-making process.

3. **Retargeting Campaigns**: Not all consumers will move from awareness to purchase immediately. Some may visit your website but leave without converting. Retargeting campaigns serve as a reminder by displaying ads to users who have previously engaged with your brand. These ads subtly encourage them to revisit your site and reconsider making a purchase.

Example: Warby Parker

The eyewear brand Warby Parker excels in the Consideration phase with its Home Try-On program. Customers can choose five frames to have shipped to their home for free, allowing them to try before they buy. This not only provides a tactile experience but also reduces the perceived risk of purchasing glasses online. Warby Parker has made it easy for consumers to gather all the information they need to feel confident in their purchase, from home trials to transparent pricing and return policies.

Stage 3: Purchase – The Moment of Truth

After careful consideration, a consumer moves to the Purchase stage, the moment they decide to buy. While getting a customer to this point is crucial, ensuring a seamless and satisfying purchasing process is equally important. Friction during checkout, unclear payment methods, or slow websites can lead to cart abandonment and lost sales.

Brands must make purchasing easy, whether online, through mobile apps, or in-store. However, the experience doesn't end at the transaction. Post-purchase engagement plays a key role in determining whether a customer becomes loyal or leaves after one purchase.

Optimizing the Purchase Experience

1. **Simple, Fast Checkout**: A streamlined checkout process reduces drop-offs. Offering guest checkout, multiple payment options, and minimizing steps to complete a purchase are essential. Amazon's one-click checkout is a prime example of how simplicity can significantly reduce cart abandonment.
2. **Personalization**: Personalized offers based on browsing history or past interactions can increase conversion rates. For example, Spotify presents customized deals to new users based on their listening preferences, creating a compelling purchase experience.
3. **Post-Purchase Communication**: Keeping customers engaged after a purchase strengthens the relationship. Brands can send thank-you emails, order updates, and related product recommendations to enhance customer satisfaction and encourage repeat business.

Example: Apple provides a seamless purchasing experience, whether online or in-store. Its website is optimized for speed, clarity, and ease of use, while retail locations offer a similarly streamlined process. The option to buy online and pick up in-store reduces friction, and Apple's post-purchase support, including product tutorials and customer service, ensures continued engagement.

Stage 4: Loyalty – Building a Long-Term Relationship

In the Loyalty stage, brands have the opportunity to turn a one-time buyer into a repeat customer and, ideally, a brand advocate. Customer retention is far more cost-effective than acquisition, and loyal customers tend to spend more over time while recommending the brand to others.

Loyalty isn't automatic; it is earned through exceptional products, personalized experiences, and continuous engagement.

Fostering Customer Loyalty

1. **Loyalty Programs**: Incentivizing repeat purchases through rewards programs builds long-term relationships. Programs like Sephora's Beauty Insider and Starbucks Rewards create a sense of exclusivity, making customers feel valued and encouraging repeat business.

2. **Post-Purchase Engagement**: Maintaining communication after a purchase fosters loyalty. Personalized email campaigns featuring special offers, product recommendations, and exclusive content keep customers engaged. Nordstrom excels at this by sending thank-you notes and invitations to exclusive events for their loyal shoppers.

3. **Exceptional Customer Service**: A standout customer service experience can transform a satisfied customer into a lifelong one. Zappos, for instance, is renowned for its customer service excellence, with representatives going above and beyond to assist shoppers, whether arranging exchanges or offering personalized recommendations.

Example: Amazon Prime exemplifies customer loyalty. By offering perks such as free two-day shipping, exclusive deals, and streaming services, Amazon creates a sense of added value beyond just purchasing products. This convenience and exclusivity foster deep loyalty, making Prime members more likely to buy from Amazon than competitors.

The Importance of Connecting the Dots

A common mistake brands make is treating each stage of the customer journey in isolation. In reality, the journey is a continuous loop, with each stage influencing the next. A positive post-purchase experience can lead to brand advocacy, bringing in new customers through word-of-mouth and restarting the cycle.

Brands must take a holistic approach, ensuring a seamless flow across all touchpoints. Consistency in experience builds trust and strengthens long-term relationships.

Takeaway

The customer journey is no longer a simple linear path but a dynamic, multi-touch experience. By understanding and optimizing each stage, Awareness, Consideration, Purchase, and Loyalty, brands can create meaningful engagements that drive long-term success. Excelling at one stage isn't enough; mastering the entire journey is key to converting one-time buyers into loyal advocates.

Chapter 7

The Importance Of Your Website In Connecting With Customers

No matter the size of your business, having an online presence is essential in today's digital landscape. Your website serves as a cornerstone of your marketing and branding strategy, acting as a powerful tool for engaging potential customers and guiding them through the buying journey. Not only does it provide an accessible platform for people to learn more about your business, but it also helps convey your brand identity, values, and the unique products or services you offer. This chapter explores the importance of establishing a professional website, particularly for mid-sized businesses and startups.

The Role of a Website in Branding and Marketing

In today's competitive market, a website is more than just a digital storefront, it is a fundamental part of your branding and marketing efforts. A well-designed website that is visually appealing and easy to navigate can effectively communicate your business's personality and core values. With the right branding and marketing strategies, your website can help you reach a wider audience and convert visitors into loyal customers. To stay ahead of the competition, investing in a high-quality website should be a top priority.

Creating a Unique Website Design to Stand Out

With countless businesses operating online, having a distinctive website is critical. Your site should not only look appealing but also reflect your brand's unique identity. Working with professional designers ensures that your website stands out visually while also being user-friendly and optimized for search engines. A memorable and engaging design leaves a lasting impression on visitors, increasing the likelihood of customer retention and brand loyalty.

Leveraging Color Psychology in Web Design

Color choices go beyond aesthetics, they influence emotions and behavior. Understanding color psychology allows you to create a more engaging and effective website. For example:

- **Blue** conveys trust, stability, and calmness, making it a great choice for financial institutions or healthcare websites.
- **Red** evokes urgency and excitement, making it ideal for call-to-action buttons.
- **Green** symbolizes growth and sustainability, making it a strong choice for eco-friendly brands. Incorporating color psychology into your web design enhances user engagement, improves the overall experience, and encourages visitors to take desired actions.

Optimizing Your Website for SEO

Simply having a website is not enough, it must be optimized for search engines to attract the right audience. SEO (Search Engine Optimization) enhances your website's visibility, credibility, and authority, ensuring it ranks higher in search results. A well-optimized site:

- Improves online discoverability
- Increases organic traffic

- Builds trust with users
- Enhances conversion rates By implementing an effective SEO strategy, businesses can significantly improve engagement and conversion rates.

Incorporating Visuals to Enhance Engagement

Visual content plays a crucial role in keeping users engaged. Research shows that people retain information better when it is presented with compelling visuals. High-quality images, infographics, and videos make your website more engaging and help establish your brand as modern and professional. By integrating well-designed visuals, you can create a dynamic and memorable browsing experience that encourages visitors to stay longer and interact more with your content.

Using Web Analytics to Measure Performance and Improve User Experience

To ensure your website is performing optimally, it is essential to track key metrics using web analytics. Analyzing data such as traffic sources, user behavior, and conversion rates provides valuable insights into:

- Which pages generate the most traffic
- Where visitors drop off
- How users navigate your site With this information, you can make informed decisions to enhance engagement, improve conversions, and drive business success.

A well-designed, strategically optimized website is one of the most valuable assets a business can have. By focusing on key elements such as unique design, color psychology, SEO, engaging visuals, and performance analytics, you can build a website that stands out, attracts visitors, and converts them into loyal customers. Taking the time to develop an effective online platform now will yield long-term benefits, strengthening your brand presence and ensuring sustainable business growth. Designing your website with the user experience in mind will set you apart in an increasingly digital world.

Why Bad UX (User Experience) Destroys Sales

Imagine this scenario: A customer scrolling through Instagram sees an influencer talking about a product that catches their eye. The influencer promises everything you have been looking for, style, convenience, and a reasonable price. Excited, they click the link to visit the brand's website. But once they arrive, they're met with slow load times, cluttered navigation, and a complicated checkout process. Frustrated and confused, they abandon their cart and leave the site, never to return. This scenario highlights the harsh reality of bad user experience (UX).

In today's digital-first marketplace, no matter how good your product is, poor UX can mean the difference between securing a sale and losing a potential lifetime customer. Consumers expect fast, intuitive, and seamless interactions with brands, and when a website or app fails to deliver, it undermines the entire experience.

The Role of UX in the Customer Journey

User experience isn't just about flashy design or the latest website features. It's about creating a frictionless journey for your customers, from the moment they land on your site to the point of purchase and beyond. A positive UX should feel effortless. When done well, it enables consumers to navigate a site, find the products or information they need, and complete a purchase without confusion or frustration.

However, when UX is done poorly, it can derail even the most interested buyers. Whether through a slow website, clunky mobile apps, hard-to-find product pages, or a confusing checkout process, bad UX frustrates consumers and drives them away.

Why UX Matters

1. **First Impressions Count** – A customer forms an impression of your website in just five seconds. If your site is slow to load, difficult to navigate, or visually unappealing, that first impression can be damaging and nearly impossible to recover from.

2. **Conversions Hinge on Simplicity** – The easier you make it for consumers to find what they want and complete a purchase, the higher your conversion rates will be. A well-designed UX reduces the number of steps in the purchasing process, minimizes distractions, and ensures customers don't feel overwhelmed.

3. **Retention Depends on Satisfaction** – Good UX doesn't just lead to an initial sale, it helps build long-term loyalty. Customers are far more likely to return to a website or app that provides a smooth, enjoyable experience. In contrast, a poor experience leads to frustration and pushes customers toward competitors offering better alternatives.

Common UX Mistakes That Destroy Sales

Many brands unknowingly sabotage their success by making UX mistakes that frustrate and alienate their customers. Let's look at some of the most common UX blunders and their impact on sales.

1. Slow Load Times

Modern consumers have little patience for slow websites. According to Google, 53% of mobile site visits are abandoned if a page takes longer than three seconds to load. In an age where consumers expect instant gratification, slow load times can be fatal for a brand.

2. Poor Mobile Optimization

Mobile commerce is no longer an afterthought, it's a dominant channel for online shopping. In 2021, mobile commerce accounted for nearly 73% of all e-commerce sales worldwide. Yet, many brands still fail to optimize their websites for mobile users. Issues such as tiny buttons, unresponsive pages, and difficult-to-navigate menus lead to high bounce rates and lost sales. Brands must ensure their websites and apps are mobile-first, not just mobile-friendly.

3. Complicated Checkout Processes

One of the biggest causes of abandoned shopping carts is a complicated or drawn-out checkout. Studies show that 69% of online shopping carts are abandoned before a purchase is completed, often due to:

- Requiring customers to create an account before purchasing.
- Asking for excessive information.
- Offering limited payment options. The more steps involved, the more likely a customer will abandon their cart.

4. Cluttered Design

An overly complicated or cluttered website can confuse customers and make it challenging to find what they want. Too many options, pop-ups, or unnecessary features can overwhelm users and increase their chances of leaving the site. Simplicity and clean design are key to keeping customers focused on their primary actions, finding a product and completing a purchase.

One common mistake brands make is the "paradox of choice." Offering too many products or variations can overwhelm customers, making them less likely to make a decision.

5. Lack of Clear CTAs (Calls to Action)

Clear calls to action guide customers through the purchasing process. Whether it's a "Buy Now" button or an "Add to Cart" prompt, effective CTAs should be prominent and easy to find. A lack of clear guidance or poorly placed buttons can lead to confusion, causing customers to exit before completing their purchase.

6. Limited Payment Options

In today's world, customers expect a variety of payment options. Whether it's credit cards, PayPal, Apple Pay, or other digital wallets, limiting payment options can cause frustration and lead to cart abandonment. The easier you make it for customers to pay, the more likely they are to complete their purchase.

7. Poor Search Functionality

For brands with extensive inventories, having an effective search function is critical. Customers who can't easily search for products by category, brand, or keyword may become frustrated and leave. Search filters that allow users to sort by price, rating, or product type can greatly enhance the shopping experience.

Real-World Examples of UX Success and Failure

Example of UX Success: Shopify

Shopify, the leading e-commerce platform, has built its brand around creating simple, intuitive, and efficient user experiences. Shopify's platform makes it incredibly easy for brands to set up online stores, offering a streamlined interface, customizable themes, and robust analytics tools.

For consumers, the shopping experience is equally smooth, with fast-loading pages, mobile optimization, and simple checkout processes. Shopify also offers built-in payment options through Shopify Payments, making transactions seamless. This simplicity has made Shopify one of the most trusted platforms for e-commerce, with over 1.75 million merchants using it worldwide.

Example of UX Failure: Forever 21's Mobile Site

Forever 21, a once-popular fast-fashion retailer, is an example of a brand that failed to prioritize UX during a critical time in retail's shift to digital. Their mobile site was slow, difficult to navigate, and poorly optimized for mobile devices. Customers complained about pages taking too long to load, cluttered design, and a confusing checkout process.

These UX issues likely contributed to a steep decline in online sales, and eventually, Forever 21 filed for bankruptcy in 2019. With most fashion consumers shifting to mobile shopping, Forever 21's lack of attention to mobile UX became a significant competitive disadvantage, especially as brands like ASOS and Zara offered smoother, more user-friendly mobile experiences.

User experience is not just about aesthetics, it's about functionality, ease, and efficiency. A seamless, intuitive UX keeps customers engaged, drives conversions, and fosters loyalty, while a poor UX can turn potential buyers away for good.

Brands that invest in optimizing their UX will see higher retention rates, increased sales, and long-term success in the digital marketplace. The key is to prioritize simplicity, speed, and clarity, ensuring that every customer's journey from browsing to buying is as effortless as possible.

How to Improve UX and Increase Sales

Now that we've identified the common pitfalls of bad UX, let's focus on how brands can improve their user experience to enhance customer satisfaction and increase sales.

1. Prioritize Speed

Speed is one of the most critical components of UX. Optimize your website or app for fast load times, especially on mobile devices. Use compressed images, optimized code, and content delivery networks (CDNs) to ensure that pages load quickly. A faster site improves user experience and significantly reduces bounce rates, keeping potential customers engaged.

2. Design for Mobile First

With most consumers shopping on mobile devices, brands must adopt a mobile-first approach. This means designing for smaller screens first and then scaling to desktop. Ensure that buttons, menus, and product images are optimized for mobile and that the checkout process is simple and easy to complete on a smartphone. Mobile responsiveness is no longer optional, it's a necessity for capturing and retaining customers.

3. Streamline the Checkout Process

The fewer steps in the checkout process, the better. Allow customers to check out as guests without requiring account creation. Minimize the amount of information needed at checkout and offer multiple payment options, including digital wallets like PayPal and Apple Pay. Consider implementing a one-click checkout option, similar to Amazon's, to reduce friction and enhance customer satisfaction. A streamlined checkout process prevents abandoned carts and increases conversions.

4. Focus on Simplicity and Clean Design

Avoid cluttered websites that overwhelm visitors with too many choices or distractions. Simplify your site design by prioritizing clear navigation and easy-to-find products. Utilize white space effectively to create a sense of calm and clarity. Ensure every element on your page serves a purpose and enhances the user experience rather than detracting from it. A clean, intuitive design builds trust and encourages visitors to stay longer.

5. Test Your UX Regularly

UX isn't a set-it-and-forget-it process. Brands need to continuously test their websites and apps to ensure they meet customer expectations. Use A/B testing to experiment with different layouts, designs, and checkout flows to determine what performs best. Regular testing and optimization can help catch potential issues before they negatively impact sales, ensuring a seamless experience for every visitor.

6. Use Data to Personalize the Experience

Personalization is a powerful tool for improving UX. By leveraging customer data to offer tailored product recommendations, exclusive deals, or customized content, you can create a more engaging and relevant shopping experience. Companies like Netflix and Amazon excel at personalizing UX by suggesting content or products based on user behavior. Implementing data-driven personalization can significantly enhance user engagement and loyalty.

Takeaway

Bad UX is one of the quickest ways to lose a customer, while great UX can turn a casual browser into a lifelong advocate. Brands that prioritize speed, simplicity, and mobile optimization while continuously testing and improving their user experience will gain a competitive edge. In today's crowded marketplace, delivering seamless, intuitive, and enjoyable experiences is key to converting interest into sales and fostering long-term customer relationships.

Chapter 8

The Importance Of Consumer Feedback And Continuous Improvement

In an era where consumers have more power and voice than ever before, feedback has become one of the most critical elements for driving business success. Consumer expectations constantly evolve, and brands that fail to adapt risk losing relevance. In this dynamic landscape, companies that actively seek feedback, listen to their customers, and respond with meaningful improvements are the ones that thrive.

The days when businesses could make assumptions about what consumers wanted are long gone. Today, data-driven decision-making and direct consumer input are essential for success. Whether through reviews, surveys, social media engagement, or real-time customer service interactions, brands have access to a wealth of information that can help them improve everything from product design to marketing strategies. However, gathering feedback is only half the equation; the real value lies in how a company uses that feedback to drive continuous improvement.

The Value of Consumer Feedback

At its core, consumer feedback is about closing the gap between a brand's perception of its products or services and the customer's actual experience. Feedback directly links the thoughts, preferences, and pain points of the people who matter most, your customers. When brands take consumer feedback seriously, they gain actionable insights into what's working, what's not, and how to improve.

Critical Benefits of Gathering Feedback

1. **Improved Products and Services:** Feedback offers direct insight into how consumers use your products or services and where improvements are needed. Customers often point out specific issues, whether functionality, usability, or design, that might not be obvious to the company. Acting on this feedback ensures you continually refine your offerings to meet customer needs.

2. **Increased Customer Loyalty:** Consumers want to feel heard. When a brand demonstrates that it values customer input and makes changes based on feedback, it builds trust and strengthens customer loyalty. People are more likely to stick with a brand that listens and acts on their suggestions.

3. **Early Problem Detection:** By consistently collecting feedback, brands can spot potential problems early. Whether it's a defect in a product, a frustrating user experience, or a gap in customer service, feedback helps companies identify issues before they escalate and negatively impact the brand's reputation.

4. **Enhanced Customer Experience:** The customer journey doesn't end after the sale. Continuous feedback helps brands understand how they can improve their products and the overall experience, from purchase to customer service to long-term engagement. A positive customer experience builds brand advocates who are more likely to recommend the brand to others.

5. **Competitive Advantage:** In highly competitive markets, those who respond to consumer needs faster and more effectively have a distinct advantage. Brands that actively collect and implement

feedback are more agile, allowing them to outpace competitors by aligning more closely with what customers want.

Channels for Gathering Consumer Feedback

Feedback can come from many different sources, and each offers unique insights into the customer's experience. The key is to use multiple channels to gather a well-rounded view of consumer sentiment and behavior. Here are the most effective ways brands can collect feedback:

1. **Online Reviews**
    Platforms like Amazon, Yelp, Google Reviews, and TripAdvisor are treasure troves of customer feedback. These public reviews give potential customers a firsthand account of other people's experiences with a brand and provide companies with a clear picture of where they excel and where improvements are needed.

2. **Surveys and Questionnaires**
    Surveys are one of the most direct ways to gather feedback. Post-purchase surveys, email questionnaires, or in-app surveys can ask specific questions about the customer's experience. Brands like Netflix often use post-interaction surveys to gauge satisfaction with customer service or product offerings.

3. **Social Media**
    Social media platforms are a goldmine for real-time feedback. Customers frequently share their thoughts, complaints, and praise on Instagram, TikTok, and Facebook. By actively monitoring social media, brands can engage with customers directly, resolve issues quickly, and gain insight into broader trends in customer sentiment.

4. **Customer Service Interactions**
    Every interaction with customer service, whether through phone calls, chat, email, or in-store visits, is an opportunity to gather feedback. Customer service reps are often on the front lines of

customer complaints and can provide valuable insights into recurring issues or emerging trends.

5. **Product Testing and Focus Groups**

   For more in-depth feedback, brands can conduct focus groups or beta-test new products. This hands-on approach allows companies to observe how consumers interact with products in real-time and gain valuable insights into how those products can be improved before they hit the market.

Real-Time Feedback and the Need for Agility

One of the most significant advantages of today's digital tools is the ability to gather real-time feedback. Brands no longer need to wait weeks or months to learn what customers think about a new product, service, or marketing campaign. With real-time feedback, companies can immediately adjust their offerings, addressing issues as they arise.

For example, when Uber first launched, it faced significant pushback from users regarding its surge pricing model. However, Uber quickly gathered and analyzed this feedback, which led to more transparent communication about surge pricing and the implementation of real-time notifications to help users make more informed decisions. This ability to act on real-time feedback improved the user experience and demonstrated that Uber was listening to its customers.

In fast-moving industries, brands that can pivot quickly based on feedback are far more likely to stay relevant and competitive. Whether tweaking a feature, refining a product, or altering a customer service policy, agility in response to consumer input is key.

How to Act on Feedback Effectively

While gathering feedback is essential, it's only valuable if brands know how to act on it. Too many companies collect data and insights but fail to make meaningful changes based on the feedback they receive. Acting on feedback requires a transparent system for analyzing data, prioritizing issues, and implementing solutions.

1. **Categorize and Prioritize Feedback**

   Not all feedback is equally actionable, and brands must learn to prioritize which issues to address first. Feedback can be categorized into major areas such as product design, user experience, and customer service, then ranked based on urgency and impact. High-priority issues, such as product defects or widespread usability complaints, should be addressed immediately, while less critical feedback, such as aesthetic preferences, can be considered for future updates.

2. **Close the Feedback Loop**

   Closing the feedback loop is one of the most important aspects of acting on feedback. This means communicating with customers who provided input and letting them know their feedback has led to specific changes. Brands that close the feedback loop demonstrate that they are actively listening, strengthening customer relationships by proving that their opinions matter.For example, Slack, the workplace messaging app, frequently gathers user feedback to guide product updates. They also close the feedback loop by announcing new features or improvements driven by customer input and thanking users for their suggestions. This practice reinforces loyalty and keeps customers engaged.

3. **Use Data to Drive Decision-Making**

   Feedback often comes in anecdotal or emotional forms, so combining it with hard data is essential. Brands should use tools like customer satisfaction (CSAT) scores, net promoter scores (NPS), and customer effort scores (CES) to quantify feedback and track improvements over time. This data-driven approach ensures that decisions are based on real insights rather than assumptions or isolated complaints.

Case Study: Starbucks and the My Starbucks Idea Platform

A prime example of a brand that mastered the art of acting on feedback is Starbucks with its "My Starbucks Idea" platform. When the platform launched in 2008, customers were invited to submit ideas for new products, store improvements, and company initiatives. Over the years, it generated over 150,000 ideas, many of which were implemented by Starbucks, including free Wi-Fi, mobile payments, and new menu items like Pumpkin Spice Lattes.

By giving customers a direct say in how the brand evolved, Starbucks created a deeper sense of engagement and loyalty. Customers felt empowered, knowing their feedback had a tangible impact on the company. This transparent and collaborative approach not only improved Starbucks' offerings but also strengthened its relationship with customers.

The Danger of Ignoring Feedback

Conversely, brands that ignore feedback risk alienating their customer base and damaging their reputation. In today's interconnected world, failing to acknowledge or mishandling feedback can lead to public backlash, negative reviews, and loss of trust.

Example: Blockbuster's Failure to Adapt

One of the most infamous examples of ignoring feedback is Blockbuster, the once-dominant video rental giant. As consumer preferences shifted toward online streaming and digital rentals, Blockbuster failed to adapt. Even though customers were moving away from physical rentals, Blockbuster doubled down on its brick-and-mortar business model, ignoring the market's changing dynamics. Meanwhile, companies like Netflix listened to consumers' desire for convenience and personalization, launching a streaming service that disrupted the entire industry. Blockbuster's failure to listen to consumer feedback and innovate led to its downfall, while Netflix became a household name.

Continuous Improvement: Never Stop Evolving

Successful brands understand that feedback and improvement are continuous processes. No matter how good a product or service is, there is always room for enhancement. Companies that embrace continuous improvement are better positioned to stay competitive and relevant over time.

Continuous improvement means never being complacent. Brands are always looking for ways to refine their products, services, and customer experiences. This process might involve regular updates to a digital platform, periodic product enhancements, or new service offerings based on customer needs.

Brands such as Tesla excel at continuous improvement. Tesla frequently pushes over-the-air vehicle updates, improving everything from autopilot performance to entertainment features. This commitment to ongoing enhancement ensures that Tesla owners always have the latest technology, making the brand feel innovative and forward-thinking.

Takeaway

Consumer feedback is no longer optional, it's essential for driving growth and building long-term loyalty. Brands that actively listen, prioritize, and act on feedback set themselves apart from competitors and position themselves for continuous improvement. In today's fast-moving world, feedback provides the insights needed to keep up with changing consumer preferences, while continuous improvement ensures that a brand never falls behind. The brands that listen are the brands that win.

Chapter 9

Marketing For The Modern Consumer: It's All About Connection

The marketing landscape has undergone a profound transformation over the past decade. Where once the focus was on driving awareness through mass advertising and pushing products to consumers, the modern consumer expects something more: connection. Today's consumers want to engage with brands that understand them, speak to their values, and offer authentic, two-way communication. This shift has been primarily driven by the rise of social media, the demand for transparency, and the desire for personalized experiences.

For brands, marketing success is no longer just about increasing reach or shouting the loudest. It's about building trust, creating relationships, and fostering a sense of community around the brand. This chapter explores how marketing strategies have evolved, why connection is the new currency, and how brands can cultivate deep, lasting customer relationships.

The Evolution of the Marketing Funnel

Traditional marketing followed a predictable path known as the marketing funnel, which moved consumers from awareness to conversion in a linear manner. Brands generated awareness through broad-reach advertising, then used promotions, discounts, or incentives to push customers down the funnel until they made a purchase. Once the sale was complete, the relationship between the brand and the customer often ended, and the focus shifted to acquiring new customers.

But that funnel no longer works in the same way. The modern marketing funnel has evolved into a loop where post-purchase engagement is just as important as the initial sale. The goal is not just to convert but to retain and engage. The new funnel looks like this:

1. **Awareness** – Brands still need to attract new customers, but this often happens through more targeted, personalized approaches like social media and influencer marketing.
2. **Consideration** – Consumers enter a research phase, where they look for reviews, watch tutorials, or seek peer recommendations before committing to a purchase.
3. **Purchase** – The customer decides to buy, but the process must be seamless and friction-free to ensure conversion.
4. **Loyalty** – Post-purchase engagement is critical to ensuring the customer returns and eventually becomes a brand advocate, helping to create a cycle of referrals and repeat business.

The key shift is that loyalty and engagement are now just as important as the initial sale. Some of the most valuable marketing occurs after the sale through ongoing relationship-building.

Storytelling: The Heart of Modern Marketing

Storytelling is one of the most effective ways to build connections with consumers. Today's consumers are drawn to brands with a compelling narrative, a clear mission, and values that resonate with their own. Storytelling humanizes a brand, making it relatable and memorable. Instead of focusing solely on product features and benefits, brands can tell stories that inspire, entertain, or educate their audience.

Why Storytelling Works

1. **Emotional Engagement** – Stories evoke emotions, and emotions drive decisions. People are more likely to connect with a brand that makes them feel something, whether it's excitement, nostalgia, inspiration, or a sense of belonging.
2. **Memorability** – Stories are easier to remember than facts. A consumer might forget a list of product features, but they're more likely to remember a brand with a compelling story about overcoming challenges, helping a community, or pursuing a higher purpose.
3. **Authenticity** – A well-told story provides context for why a brand exists and what it stands for. It gives consumers a sense of who the people behind the brand are, making the company feel more authentic and human.

Example: Nike's "You Can't Stop Us" Campaign

Nike's "You Can't Stop Us" campaign (2020-2021) was a masterclass in brand storytelling, leveraging emotion, relatability, and cultural relevance.

Why It Worked:

- **Emotional Connection** – The ad used a split-screen format, seamlessly blending 36 different sports and athletes to showcase resilience, unity, and perseverance. It resonated deeply in a time of global uncertainty.
- **Cultural Relevance** – It addressed themes like the pandemic, racial justice, gender equality, and the return of sports.
- **Brand Values Alignment** – Nike has long stood for perseverance, equality, and human potential. The campaign reinforced its brand identity authentically.
- **Viral Impact** – The video racked up millions of views within hours, sparking conversations and solidifying Nike's position as a cultural leader.

Key Takeaways for Other Brands:

- **Authenticity Matters** – Customers connect with brands that stand for something beyond just selling products.
- **Emotional Storytelling is Key** – Data and facts are important, but emotional, human-centric storytelling drives engagement.
- **Cultural Relevance Enhances Connection** – Addressing real-world events and struggles makes a brand feel more human.

This campaign was a benchmark in using storytelling to inspire, engage, and create lasting brand loyalty. Brands looking to craft a similar narrative-driven campaign should prioritize authenticity and emotional engagement.

The Shift to Personalization

Another major factor in modern marketing is the shift toward personalization. Today's consumers expect brands to understand their individual preferences, needs, and behaviors. With the wealth of data available, brands can now create tailored experiences that make consumers feel valued and understood.

Why Personalization Matters

1. **Relevance:** Consumers are inundated with content daily, and personalization helps brands cut through the noise. When a brand delivers a personalized experience, whether through product recommendations, targeted emails, or customized ads, it feels more relevant to the consumer, increasing engagement and conversions.

2. **Customer Satisfaction:** Personalization enhances the customer experience by making interactions more seamless and intuitive. Consumers are more likely to purchase from brands that offer relevant products or services tailored to their needs, reducing friction in the buying process and increasing satisfaction.

3. **Increased Loyalty:** Personalized experiences foster deeper connections, making consumers feel valued. Brands that continually refine personalization efforts build trust and long-term customer loyalty.

Example: Spotify's Personalized Playlists

Spotify's data-driven personalization strategy is a standout example. The platform curates playlists like *Discover Weekly* and *Daily Mix* based on user listening habits, making recommendations feel uniquely tailored. This approach increases user engagement and strengthens brand loyalty, demonstrating the power of personalization in any industry.

Community-Building: Creating a Space for Consumers to Connect

Building a community around a brand fosters deeper consumer engagement and advocacy. Successful communities provide a space where customers feel a sense of belonging and shared purpose, leading to organic brand growth.

Why Community Matters

1. **Shared Identity:** Consumers want to be part of something larger than themselves. When brands create communities based on shared interests, values, or goals, they foster emotional connections and brand affinity.
2. **Peer Support and Advocacy:** Community members often assist one another, answer questions, and offer recommendations. This peer support builds trust and turns customers into brand advocates.
3. **Brand Longevity:** Unlike individual campaigns or products, communities create long-term brand affinity that outlasts market shifts or business model changes.

Example: Peloton's Fitness Community

Peloton has built one of the most engaged brand communities by integrating social connectivity into its fitness ecosystem. Riders join challenges, celebrate milestones, and interact with instructors and fellow members, making workouts feel like shared experiences. This sense of belonging fosters customer loyalty and transforms buyers into passionate advocates.

The Role of Social Media in Building Connections

Social media enables brands to connect with consumers in real time, creating opportunities for two-way engagement, storytelling, and community building.

Social Media Strategies for Connection

1. **Engage, Don't Just Broadcast:** Brands should focus on conversations rather than just pushing messages. Responding to comments, answering questions, and acknowledging feedback demonstrate that a brand values its customers. Wendy's, for example, has built a strong presence through witty, relatable social media interactions.

2. **Use Visual Storytelling:** Platforms like Instagram and TikTok thrive on visual content. Brands that leverage high-quality imagery, videos, and user-generated content can create memorable experiences that resonate emotionally with consumers.

3. **Leverage User-Generated Content (UGC):** Encouraging customers to share their experiences fosters authenticity. Brands like GoPro and Lululemon actively feature real customers in campaigns, enhancing credibility and engagement.

The Importance of Transparency and Authenticity

Consumers today are more skeptical of brands than ever before. They value transparency and authenticity, rewarding brands that communicate honestly and align actions with values.

How to Build Authentic Connections

1. **Be Transparent:** Whether sharing behind-the-scenes content, admitting mistakes, or discussing challenges, transparency builds trust. Patagonia, for example, has cultivated a loyal following by openly discussing its sustainability efforts.
2. **Stay True to Your Values:** Consumers can sense when a brand is disingenuous. Successful brands consistently uphold their values, even when faced with difficult business decisions.
3. **Listen and Respond:** Building connections is a two-way street. Brands that actively listen to customer feedback and implement meaningful changes foster deeper relationships and long-term loyalty.

Takeaway

Modern marketing is about more than just selling, it's about connection. Consumers seek brands that understand, value, and engage them on a deeper level. Successful brands prioritize storytelling, personalization, community-building, and authenticity to foster long-lasting relationships. In today's competitive landscape, connection is the new currency of marketing, and those who master it will not only drive sales but also earn customer loyalty and trust.

Chapter 10

Selling To The Skeptical Consumer

The modern consumer is skeptical. Over the years, a barrage of exaggerated claims, misleading advertising, and corporate scandals has eroded brand trust. Today's buyers are cautious, hyper-aware, and critical of marketing messages. They question the validity of every claim, compare multiple sources of information before making decisions, and expect brands to prove their worth before they make a purchase.

In this environment, traditional sales tactics no longer work. Flashy promises, pushy ads, and hollow claims are met with resistance or outright rejection. To succeed in selling to today's skeptical consumer, brands must work harder to build trust, provide transparency, and offer solid proof that their products or services deliver on their promises.

Why Consumers Are Skeptical

There are several key reasons why consumers have become more skeptical in recent years. Understanding these factors can help brands tailor their messaging and approach to connect with this cautious audience.

Overload of Information and Options

The sheer volume of information available to consumers today has made them more discerning. With just a few clicks, they can compare prices, read reviews, and access product details from multiple brands. They are bombarded with choices and marketing messages at every turn, making it difficult to discern what is real and what is exaggerated. This information overload has contributed to skepticism, as consumers now approach marketing claims cautiously and seek validation before making a decision.

A History of Deceptive Advertising

The marketing industry has a long history of deceptive advertising. Whether it's miracle diet pills, "too good to be true" deals, or misleading claims about product benefits, consumers have been misled too many times. This history has created a deep-rooted mistrust of brands, leading consumers to question every promise and demand proof before they believe it.

The Rise of Social Media and Influencers

While social media has allowed consumers to be more informed, it has also led to skepticism about who to trust. The rise of influencers, some of whom endorse products purely for financial gain, has made consumers wary of sponsored content. Authenticity is often questioned, and many buyers are now more critical of paid endorsements, looking instead for genuine recommendations from sources they trust.

Corporate Scandals and Broken Trust

Corporate scandals, from product recalls to data breaches, have had a lasting impact on consumer trust. Whether it's the Volkswagen emissions scandal, Facebook's mishandling of user data, or fast fashion's environmental damage, consumers have seen too many examples of brands failing to live up to their promises. As a result, they approach new brands with skepticism, questioning whether they are as ethical, sustainable, or reliable as they claim to be.

The Importance of Social Proof

One of the most effective ways to combat consumer skepticism is through social proof. Social proof refers to the influence that the actions and opinions of others have on our behavior. This psychological phenomenon leads us to trust a product or service more when others have had positive experiences.

In an age of skepticism, social proof is a powerful tool for building trust because it validates a brand's claims externally. Consumers are far more likely to trust the opinions of fellow customers, friends, or independent reviewers than they are to believe a brand's marketing.

Forms of Social Proof

1. **Customer Reviews**: Reviews are one of the most trusted forms of social proof. Research shows that 92% of consumers read online reviews before making a purchase, and 84% trust online reviews as much as personal recommendations. Brands should actively encourage customer reviews and showcase them prominently on websites and product pages to build trust.

2. **Testimonials and Case Studies**: Featuring real stories from satisfied customers or demonstrating how a product or service solved a specific problem makes a brand's claims more believable. These personal narratives add a human element and help potential customers relate to the product.

3. **Third-Party Endorsements**: Whether it's an award from a respected organization, a review from a well-known publication, or an endorsement from an industry expert, third-party validation lends credibility. Consumers are more likely to trust a brand when independent sources recognize it.

4. **User-Generated Content (UGC)**: UGC is an authentic form of social proof that brands can leverage. When customers share photos or videos of themselves using a product, it feels more genuine than traditional ads. Brands like Glossier and GoPro

excel in this area, regularly featuring UGC on their social media platforms and websites.

Transparency: The Antidote to Skepticism

In a world where consumers are inundated with information, brands can combat skepticism most effectively by embracing transparency. Modern buyers appreciate brands that are open, honest, and willing to share details about their processes, pricing, and challenges. Transparency demonstrates that a brand has nothing to hide, building trust and reassuring consumers.

How Brands Can Build Transparency

1. **Be Open About Product Limitations**: No product is perfect, and consumers know this. Brands that are upfront about their product's limitations earn credibility. For example, if a laptop has a shorter battery life than competitors, acknowledging this while emphasizing its other strengths (such as performance or design) makes the brand seem more trustworthy. Transparency about imperfections shows that the brand is honest.

2. **Show Behind-the-Scenes Content**: Consumers want to see the people and processes behind a brand. Sharing behind-the-scenes content, such as a factory tour, interviews with employees, or details about product development, humanizes the brand and builds trust. This level of openness makes consumers feel like they are part of the journey and reinforces transparency.

3. **Disclose Pricing and Fees Clearly**: Hidden fees or complicated pricing models are major turn-offs for skeptical consumers. Brands that provide clear, upfront pricing, including any potential additional costs (such as shipping or taxes), reduce friction in the buying process and build trust. Warby Parker, for instance, offers transparent pricing on all their eyewear, so customers know exactly what they're paying before making a purchase.

4. **Address Mistakes Head-On**: Every brand makes mistakes, whether it's a defective product, a customer service failure, or a public relations misstep. What sets trustworthy brands apart is how they respond. Brands that take ownership of their mistakes, apologize, and outline clear improvement steps can build stronger trust than those that try to cover up or downplay issues. JetBlue, for example, has built a reputation for customer-centric service by acknowledging and apologizing for flight delays and cancellations, often offering compensation without being asked.

Building Trust Through Consistency

Trust isn't built overnight; it is earned through consistent actions over time. For skeptical consumers, making a single good impression is not enough. Brands must continually prove their reliability by delivering on promises, maintaining high standards, and acting with integrity.

Keys to Building Trust Through Consistency

1. **Consistency Across All Channels**: Whether through a website, social media, or in-store experience, consistency is key. Consumers expect the same level of quality, service, and communication across all platforms. Inconsistencies in pricing, customer service, or product quality can erode trust and feed into consumer skepticism.
2. **Deliver on Promises**: One of the quickest ways to lose trust is by over-promising and under-delivering. Brands that make bold claims about product performance, delivery times, or customer service must ensure they can back them up. Consistently fulfilling promises is essential to earning and maintaining trust.
3. **Provide Excellent Customer Service**: Customer service is often where trust is built or broken. Consumers want to feel confident that if something goes wrong, the brand will make it right. Prompt, courteous, and effective customer service builds

trust and loyalty. Zappos, for example, is renowned for going above and beyond to meet customers' needs, fostering a strong sense of trust.

4. **Maintain High Standards**: Trust is reinforced through the consistent quality of a brand's products or services. Brands that cut corners to reduce costs risk alienating their customer base. By prioritizing high standards in product development, ethical sourcing, and sustainability efforts, brands solidify their reputation for reliability.

Case Study: Patagonia's Transparency and Trust

Patagonia has excelled at selling to skeptical consumers by being transparent, honest, and mission-driven. One of its most famous campaigns, "Don't Buy This Jacket," encouraged consumers to reconsider purchasing new products, emphasizing sustainability and responsible consumption.

Beyond marketing, Patagonia remains transparent about its supply chain, labor practices, and environmental impact. The company regularly publishes reports detailing its footprint, sharing both successes and areas for improvement. This level of openness has helped Patagonia build a loyal customer base that trusts its commitment to sustainability.

By consistently delivering high-quality products while being candid about its sustainability challenges, Patagonia has earned the trust of consumers who care about ethical and environmental responsibility.

The Role of Proof: Showing, Not Just Telling

In a world where consumers are skeptical of marketing claims, proof is essential. It's not enough for a brand to say it's the best, consumers want evidence. Brands that provide concrete proof of their claims are far more likely to earn trust.

Ways to Provide Proof

1. **Demonstrate Product Performance**: Brands should offer tangible evidence of product effectiveness, such as demo videos, product trials, or independent test results. Dyson, for instance, showcases the science behind its products, demonstrating their performance compared to competitors.

2. **Leverage Data**: Statistics add credibility to a brand's claims. Whether through customer satisfaction ratings, return rates, or performance metrics, data provides compelling proof. Peloton, for example, shares statistics about the number of rides taken and calories burned by users to reinforce its product's effectiveness.

3. **Offer Guarantees**: Guarantees or warranties demonstrate a brand's confidence in its products. Risk-free trials and money-back guarantees ease consumer skepticism and signal reliability.

Takeaway

Selling to skeptical consumers requires a shift from traditional marketing tactics to strategies that prioritize trust, transparency, and proof. In an era where buyers are hyper-aware of misleading claims, successful brands are those that back up promises, offer social proof, and build long-term trust through consistency.

While skepticism is high, it is not insurmountable. Brands that listen to consumers, act with integrity, and continuously prove their worth will win the loyalty of even the most cautious buyers.

Chapter 11

E-Commerce Giants:
Selling In A Marketplace World

It's hard to overstate the impact of e-commerce giants like Amazon, eBay, and Etsy on modern consumer behavior. These platforms have redefined convenience, providing consumers easy access to millions of products at competitive prices, often delivered within days or even hours. For many businesses, these marketplaces offer unparalleled reach and the ability to tap into a global customer base with minimal upfront costs.

But while e-commerce giants provide significant opportunities, they also come with unique challenges. Brands must compete with thousands of other sellers, often racing to the bottom in pricing while navigating strict platform rules. Furthermore, building a brand identity on these platforms can be difficult when you're just one of many options in a sea of competitors.

In this chapter, we'll explore how brands can leverage these marketplaces effectively while avoiding the pitfalls of over-reliance and loss of identity.

The Power of Marketplaces: Why Brands Flock to Amazon, eBay, and Etsy

E-commerce platforms have revolutionized retail by allowing anyone, from established brands to independent artisans, to sell their products to a global audience. The appeal of these marketplaces lies in their scale, convenience, and built-in trust.

Massive Reach

Amazon, the largest e-commerce platform in the world, has over 300 million active users globally. For a small business or an emerging brand, getting a product in front of such a vast audience is a game-changer. The same is true for eBay and Etsy, which provide access to millions of buyers actively searching for specific products.

This reach is one of the main reasons brands flock to marketplaces. Instead of spending heavily on advertising and driving traffic to their own website, they can tap into the millions of customers already browsing these platforms.

Built-in Infrastructure

One of the biggest advantages of selling on marketplaces like Amazon or eBay is their built-in infrastructure. These platforms handle much of the logistics, from payment processing to shipping (via programs like Fulfillment by Amazon (FBA)), making it easier for brands to scale without needing to manage all the complexities of e-commerce operations internally. Additionally, platforms like Etsy provide a ready-made storefront, allowing creators and sellers to focus more on product development and marketing rather than web development or backend logistics.

Consumer Trust

Consumers tend to trust marketplaces like Amazon and eBay because of their reputation for security, customer service, and reliable delivery. Buyers know that if they have an issue with a product or a seller, the platform will often provide support or refunds. This level of trust makes consumers more likely to purchase from a new or unknown seller on a marketplace than from an independent website.

Challenges of Selling on Marketplaces

While marketplaces offer immense opportunities, they also come with significant challenges. To succeed, brands must navigate various hurdles, from fierce competition to platform fees.

Intense Competition

The sheer volume of sellers on platforms like Amazon means fierce competition. Amazon alone has over 2 million sellers worldwide, each vying for visibility and sales. This competition creates a race to the bottom in pricing, with many sellers forced to lower their prices to remain competitive, often cutting into margins. Competing on price alone isn't sustainable for brands that want to stand out.

Additionally, marketplaces favor top-performing products in search results, creating a snowball effect where best-sellers gain more visibility and, thus, more sales. Breaking into this cycle is a challenge for new or smaller brands.

Loss of Brand Control

One of the most significant downsides to selling on a marketplace is the lack of control over brand presentation. Marketplaces are designed to showcase products, not brands. On Amazon, for instance, the product page is standardized across sellers, meaning your brand has limited visibility beyond the product itself. This makes building a distinct brand identity or creating a lasting connection with customers difficult.

For sellers on Etsy or eBay, the platform dictates the user experience and design, which may not align with a brand's unique aesthetic or messaging. While these platforms offer some customization options, brands still have limited control over how their products are presented. Amazon does provide the ability to build a brand storefront and A+ Pages to provide additional information about your brand and product.

Platform Fees and Profit Margins

Marketplaces charge fees for every sale, which can significantly reduce profit margins. Amazon, for example, charges referral fees (usually between 6-15% of the sale price) and additional costs for those using Fulfillment by Amazon (FBA). For brands with thin margins, these fees can make it difficult to turn a profit.

Additionally, sellers are often pressured to participate in marketplace promotions, such as Prime Day or Etsy sales events, which usually involve offering steep discounts. While these promotions can boost sales volume, they may also lead to reduced profit margins and attract bargain hunters rather than long-term loyal customers.

How to Succeed on E-commerce Marketplaces

Despite the challenges, many brands have succeeded on platforms like Amazon, eBay, and Etsy by implementing innovative strategies. Here's how brands can maximize their marketplace presence while mitigating the downsides.

Differentiate Your Product

Given the intense competition on marketplaces, standing out requires more than just a competitive price. Successful brands differentiate their products through unique features, premium quality, or outstanding customer service. For example, brands like Anker (which sells tech accessories on Amazon) have built a loyal following by offering consistently reliable, well-designed, and competitively priced products.

Additionally, focusing on niche markets can help brands carve out a space for themselves. On platforms like Etsy, where handmade and custom products are popular, sellers who offer highly specialized or personalized items can attract a dedicated customer base with less direct competition.

Optimize Product Listings

Optimizing product listings for marketplace algorithms is critical to visibility and sales. This process involves using search engine optimization (SEO) tactics, such as including relevant keywords in product titles and descriptions, providing high-quality images, and ensuring that all product information is complete and accurate.

For instance, Amazon's A9 algorithm determines which products appear at the top of search results. Brands that optimize their listings for this algorithm by using relevant keywords, offering competitive pricing, and generating positive reviews can improve their chances of ranking higher and driving more traffic to their products.

Encourage Reviews

Customer reviews are among the most powerful forms of social proof, especially on marketplaces. Positive reviews can significantly boost a product's visibility and credibility, while negative reviews can quickly harm sales. Brands should actively encourage satisfied customers to leave reviews and respond to negative feedback promptly to demonstrate their commitment to customer service.

Programs like Amazon Vine (which allows brands to provide products to trusted reviewers in exchange for feedback) can help new sellers generate reviews more quickly. For sellers on Etsy or eBay, offering exceptional customer service and following up with customers post-purchase can also encourage reviews.

Invest in Advertising

Marketplace advertising is an essential strategy for boosting visibility in a crowded space. Platforms like Amazon and Etsy offer sponsored product ads, which allow sellers to pay for higher placement in search results. While this can be costly, competing in highly competitive categories is often necessary.

Successful marketplace sellers often reinvest a portion of their profits into advertising to maintain visibility and drive sales. However, tracking the return on investment (ROI) is essential to ensure that ad spend isn't cutting into margins.

Leverage Fulfillment Services

Using marketplace fulfillment services, such as Amazon's Fulfillment by Amazon (FBA), can help sellers scale more quickly by outsourcing storage, shipping, and customer service. FBA sellers are also eligible for Prime shipping, which can increase the likelihood of a sale, as many Amazon customers prioritize Prime-eligible products for their fast delivery.

However, FBA comes with additional fees, so brands must weigh the cost-benefit of using these services versus handling fulfillment in-house.

Avoiding Over-Reliance on Marketplaces

While marketplaces offer immense opportunities, over-reliance on platforms like Amazon or eBay can be risky. Many brands fall into the trap of depending solely on marketplace sales, which can be dangerous if the platform changes its algorithms, policies, or fees. Worse, platforms have been known to suspend seller accounts or limit listings without warning, which can devastate a business that relies entirely on one marketplace for sales.

Build a Strong Direct-to-Consumer (DTC) Channel

One of the most important strategies for avoiding over-reliance on marketplaces is to develop a strong direct-to-consumer (DTC) channel. This allows brands to build customer relationships, control the brand experience, and avoid marketplace fees. A well-designed DTC website gives brands complete control over how products are presented and allows for better data collection and customer insights.

Successful marketplace sellers like Allbirds and Casper have built strong DTC channels while maintaining a marketplace presence. By focusing on branding, storytelling, and customer experience on their platforms, they ensure they aren't solely dependent on marketplace traffic.

Use Marketplaces as a Complement, Not a Core Strategy

Instead of using marketplaces as the sole sales channel, brands should treat them as a complement to their overall strategy. Marketplaces can be a great way to reach new customers and boost sales volume, but they should be just one part of a diversified sales strategy. Brands that balance marketplace presence with a strong DTC offering are better positioned to weather changes in the marketplace ecosystem.

Capture Customer Data

One downside of selling on marketplaces is that brands often have limited access to customer data. To build long-term customer relationships, brands should find ways to capture data outside of the marketplace. This can include offering special promotions, encouraging customers to sign up for newsletters, or directing customers to the brand's website for exclusive content or offers.

By capturing customer data, brands can develop more personalized marketing strategies, build loyalty programs, and engage with customers directly, helping to reduce reliance on marketplaces over time.

Takeaway

E-commerce marketplaces like Amazon, eBay, and Etsy have fundamentally changed the retail landscape, offering brands unprecedented access to a global audience. While the opportunities are immense, so are the challenges, intense competition, loss of brand control, and marketplace fees. Brands that succeed in this space differentiate their products, optimize their listings, and balance marketplace presence with a strong direct-to-consumer strategy. By leveraging marketplaces as part of a broader strategy, brands can build sustainable success in a marketplace-driven world rather than becoming over-reliant on them.

Chapter 12

The Value Of Customer Loyalty: Turning Buyers Into Advocates

Acquiring new customers can be costly and time-consuming. The true power of a successful brand lies in its ability to turn one-time buyers into loyal customers. Even more valuable are those loyal customers who go beyond repeat purchases to become brand advocates, individuals who actively promote your products, share their positive experiences with others, and help grow your business organically.

Building customer loyalty isn't just about delivering a good product; it's about creating an exceptional experience that keeps customers returning and encourages them to spread the word. In this chapter, we'll explore why customer loyalty is so valuable, how brands can cultivate it, and the key strategies to transform loyal customers into brand advocates.

Why Customer Loyalty Matters

For many businesses, a significant portion of revenue comes not from new customers but from repeat buyers. Studies show that existing customers are 50% more likely to try new products and spend 31% more than new customers. Additionally, loyal customers are more likely to recommend a brand to others, amplifying word-of-mouth marketing.

Key Benefits of Customer Loyalty

1. **Increased Lifetime Value (LTV):** Loyal customers tend to make frequent purchases and have a higher average order value than one-time buyers. This increases their overall lifetime value, making them more profitable over time. A repeat customer may spend more on your brand over several years than dozens of one-time customers combined.

2. **Lower Acquisition Costs:** Acquiring new customers is expensive. In fact, acquiring a new customer can cost 5 to 25 times more than retaining an existing one. By focusing on building loyalty, brands can reduce customer acquisition costs and increase profitability.

3. **Organic Growth through Word-of-Mouth:** Satisfied customers are more likely to recommend your brand to friends, family, and social networks. This form of marketing is incredibly valuable because it is authentic and trustworthy. People are more likely to trust recommendations from friends and peers than traditional advertising.

4. **Brand Advocacy and Reputation Protection:** Brand advocates love your product and are willing to defend your brand during times of criticism. When your brand faces negative reviews or public backlash, loyal customers can act as defenders, sharing their positive experiences and helping mitigate reputational damage.

Building Customer Loyalty: Key Strategies

Creating customer loyalty requires a consistent, engaging experience that makes customers feel valued and appreciated. Below are some key strategies brands can use to foster loyalty and build long-term customer relationships.

Personalization

Personalization is one of the most powerful ways to build loyalty. Today's consumers expect brands to understand their preferences, anticipate their needs, and offer tailored experiences. Personalization goes beyond just addressing the customer by name; it involves creating relevant recommendations, personalized offers, and tailored content that speaks to each customer's unique interests.

Example: Netflix

Netflix is a master of personalization. Using advanced algorithms, Netflix analyzes each user's viewing history, preferences, and behavior to offer tailored recommendations. This level of personalization makes users feel understood and appreciated, leading to higher engagement and loyalty. By providing personalized movie and TV show suggestions, Netflix ensures users keep returning for more.

Loyalty Programs

Loyalty programs effectively incentivize repeat purchases by rewarding customers for continued engagement. These programs offer points, discounts, or exclusive perks, encouraging customers to purchase more while creating a sense of belonging and exclusivity.

Example: Sephora's Beauty Insider Program

Sephora's Beauty Insider Program is one of the most successful loyalty programs in the retail space. The program offers three tiers, Insider, VIB, and Rouge, each with increasing rewards based on spending. Members earn points for every purchase, which can be redeemed for products, and higher-tier members receive exclusive perks like free shipping, early access to sales, and special gifts. This tiered system encourages customers to spend more to unlock greater rewards, fostering deep loyalty.

Outstanding Customer Service

Excellent customer service is a cornerstone of loyalty. When customers have a positive experience with a brand, whether it's a quick resolution to a problem, a helpful representative, or an unexpected act of kindness, they are more likely to remain loyal. Brands that go above and beyond in customer service can turn an ordinary transaction into a memorable experience.

Example: Chewy

One standout example of an eCommerce brand with legendary customer service and deep customer loyalty is Chewy. The online pet supply retailer has built an incredibly devoted customer base through exceptional service and personalized experiences.

Chewy is known for its 24/7 customer support, providing quick, empathetic, and helpful responses at any time of day. The company goes beyond standard service by sending handwritten notes, birthday cards for pets, and even flowers in response to pet losses, creating an emotional bond with customers that extends far beyond transactions.

Chewy also offers hassle-free returns and refunds, often issuing refunds without requiring customers to send back items, demonstrating a high level of trust. Their fast shipping and seamless ordering process ensure pet owners always have what they need when they need it. Customers frequently receive surprise gifts, holiday cards, and special care packages, further reinforcing their connection to the brand.

One of the most touching aspects of Chewy's service is its approach to pet loss support. When a customer loses a pet, Chewy often sends flowers and condolence messages, showing genuine care and compassion. This relentless focus on personalized customer service has created exceptional brand loyalty, strong word-of-mouth referrals, and repeat purchase behavior. Many customers share their heartwarming experiences on social media, amplifying Chewy's reputation as a caring brand. By consistently delivering unexpected delight and proactive service, Chewy has positioned itself as not just an eCommerce retailer but a trusted partner in pet ownership.

Consistent Communication and Engagement

Brands that maintain regular, meaningful communication with their customers are more likely to build long-term loyalty. Email marketing, social media engagement, and SMS marketing can keep customers informed about new products, special offers, and company updates. However, the key is to provide value in these communications rather than bombarding customers with irrelevant or overly promotional content.

Example: Glossier

Glossier, a beauty brand, has built a loyal following by regularly engaging with its customers on social media. Glossier's presence feels authentic, personal, and conversational, often featuring user-generated content and real customer testimonials. The brand also uses email marketing to share product tips, tutorials, and personalized offers, fostering a sense of community that keeps customers engaged between purchases.

Exclusive Offers and VIP Treatment

Consumers love feeling like they're receiving special treatment. Offering exclusive discounts, early access to new products, or VIP experiences can make customers feel valued and appreciated. When customers perceive themselves as part of an exclusive club, they are more likely to remain loyal and advocate for the brand.

Example: American Express

American Express has built its loyalty around exclusive offers and perks for its cardholders. From early access to concert tickets to airport lounge access and luxury travel benefits, American Express offers VIP treatment that sets it apart. This exclusivity fosters deep customer loyalty, making membership feel like a lifestyle rather than just a financial product.

Turning Loyal Customers into Advocates

Once a brand has built a loyal customer base, the next step is to turn those customers into advocates who actively promote the brand. Advocates are more than just repeat buyers; they are passionate fans who leave positive reviews, share experiences, and contribute to word-of-mouth marketing.

Encourage Reviews and Testimonials

Happy customers are often willing to leave reviews but may need encouragement. Brands can facilitate this by sending follow-up emails after purchases, requesting reviews, or offering incentives like discounts or points for feedback. Positive reviews build trust with potential buyers and give advocates a platform to share their enthusiasm.

Example: Amazon

Amazon actively encourages reviews by sending follow-up emails requesting feedback. By offering a simple, friction-free review process, Amazon has built a massive product review database, providing authentic social proof that helps future buyers make informed decisions.

Build a Referral Program

Referral programs are a proven way to turn loyal customers into brand advocates. These programs reward customers for referring friends or family, often offering discounts or bonuses for successful referrals. A well-designed referral program incentivizes customers to spread the word and brings in high-quality leads who are more likely to convert.

Example: Dropbox

Dropbox's referral program is a textbook example of successful referral marketing. By offering additional storage space to both the referrer and the new user, Dropbox encouraged massive organic growth. This simple yet powerful incentive helped Dropbox grow from 100,000 users to 4 million users in just 15 months, all through word-of-mouth advocacy.

Create Shareable Content

Encouraging customers to share their experiences on social media is another powerful way to build advocacy. Brands that create engaging, shareable content, such as social media challenges, user-generated content campaigns, or product unboxings, make it easy for loyal customers to spread the word.

Example: Peloton

Peloton has successfully turned its users into advocates by fostering a strong community and encouraging riders to share their workout experiences. Members frequently post milestones, leaderboard achievements, and instructor interactions on social media, creating an organic ripple effect that draws in new customers inspired by the community's passion.

Offer Recognition and Rewards for Advocacy

Recognizing and rewarding top advocates strengthens relationships and encourages ongoing promotion. Brands can acknowledge loyal customers through exclusive rewards, public shoutouts, or recognition in newsletters.

Example: Starbucks

Starbucks' Rewards program highlights its most engaged customers by featuring them in marketing campaigns and offering incentives for social media engagement. By encouraging customers to post about their Starbucks experiences with branded hashtags, Starbucks cultivates brand advocacy while making loyal customers feel valued.

Case Study: Apple's Cultivated Loyalty and Advocacy

Apple is one of the most iconic examples of a brand that has successfully cultivated loyalty and advocacy. Apple's ecosystem, from iPhones to MacBooks to AirPods, creates a seamless user experience that keeps customers invested. However, its loyalty goes beyond products;

Apple fosters emotional connections with customers through its stores, events, and marketing.

Apple's emphasis on innovation, exclusivity, and design excellence makes users feel like they are part of an elite group. This sense of exclusivity fosters deep loyalty, as users eagerly line up for new product launches, defend the brand in discussions, and promote Apple to others. By consistently delivering exceptional experiences, Apple has built one of the most dedicated customer bases in the world, achieving organic, word-of-mouth growth that far exceeds traditional advertising efforts.

Takeaway

Customer loyalty is one of the most valuable assets a brand can cultivate. Loyal customers don't just buy, they return, recommend, and advocate for the brand. By focusing on personalization, offering exceptional customer service, and building engaging loyalty programs, brands can foster long-term relationships that lead to sustainable growth. Turning loyal customers into advocates amplifies impact, driving organic growth through word-of-mouth marketing. In today's competitive market, the brands that prioritize loyalty and advocacy are the ones that will thrive.

Chapter 13

The Art Of
Storytelling In Marketing

The Power of Storytelling in Marketing

In today's marketing landscape, facts and figures alone are no longer enough to capture consumers' hearts. While product features and benefits are important, they often lack the emotional resonance that drives consumer behavior. Storytelling has emerged as one of the most powerful tools brands can use to engage their audience on a deeper level. By weaving compelling narratives, brands can communicate their values, mission, and personality in a way that resonates emotionally, creating memorable experiences that inspire loyalty and advocacy.

At its core, storytelling is about making a connection. For centuries, stories have been used to convey messages, share experiences, and build relationships. In marketing, this age-old tradition is more relevant than ever. Whether through advertising, content marketing, or social media, brands that tell compelling stories are more likely to forge lasting relationships with their customers.

Why Storytelling Matters in Marketing

Storytelling goes beyond simply communicating what a product does; it tells consumers why the brand exists, what it stands for, and why it matters to them personally. Stories evoke emotion, and emotion drives action. Here's why storytelling has become an essential part of successful marketing:

Emotional Connection

Consumers are more likely to engage with brands that evoke emotions. Emotions are powerful motivators, whether joy, inspiration, nostalgia, or empathy. A well-crafted story can make a brand feel more human, relatable, and relevant, helping to create a bond that goes beyond the transaction.

Memorability

Facts and statistics are often forgotten, but stories are remembered. The human brain is wired to remember stories more easily than isolated bits of information. When a brand tells a story, it's more likely to stick with the audience, making the brand more memorable.

Differentiation

In a crowded marketplace where consumers are bombarded with ads and content, storytelling helps brands stand out. A compelling narrative gives a brand a unique voice, helping it differentiate itself from competitors that may offer similar products or services.

Authenticity

Authenticity is a key ingredient in successful storytelling. Today's consumers are skeptical of marketing tactics that feel forced or insincere. Storytelling allows brands to share their origins, values, and mission in a genuine way, helping to build trust and credibility.

The Elements of Effective Storytelling

Great storytelling is an art form, and while there's no one-size-fits-all formula, there are several key elements that every successful brand story should have. These elements help structure the narrative in a way that resonates with the audience and leads them on a journey.

A Clear Purpose

Every brand story should have a clear purpose or message. What does the brand stand for? What problem is it trying to solve? Whether advocating for sustainability, innovation, or community, the story's purpose should align with the brand's values and mission. A story without a clear purpose will feel aimless and fail to connect with the audience.

A Relatable Hero

Every good story has a hero; in brand storytelling, that hero is often the customer. By putting the customer at the story's center, brands can show how their products or services improve their lives, solve their problems, or help them achieve their goals. The story's hero should be someone the audience can relate to, whether a struggling entrepreneur, a parent juggling responsibilities, or an adventurer seeking new experiences.

A Challenge or Conflict

In storytelling, conflict creates tension and drives the narrative forward. For brands, the conflict is often the problem that the customer is facing, whether it's needing better sleep, finding time to exercise, or reducing environmental impact. By presenting the problem clearly, the brand can position itself as the solution, providing the hero (the customer) with the tools to overcome the challenge.

A Resolution

A great story needs a satisfying resolution. In brand storytelling, the resolution is the point where the brand's product or service helps the hero overcome the conflict or challenge. This story doesn't have to be a hard sell. It's more about showing how the brand empowers the customer to succeed. The resolution should leave the audience feeling inspired, motivated, or reassured that they can achieve the same success.

Authenticity and Emotion

Authenticity is crucial in storytelling. The narrative should feel genuine, not manufactured or overly polished. Brands that share real stories, whether through customer testimonials, behind-the-scenes content, or personal anecdotes from the founders, are more likely to build trust with their audience. Additionally, tapping into emotion, whether happiness, empathy, or inspiration, helps make the story more engaging and memorable.

How to Craft a Compelling Brand Narrative

Crafting a compelling brand narrative requires a deep understanding of the brand's values, mission, and audience. It's about telling a story that resonates with the audience's emotions and aspirations while staying true to the brand's identity. Here's how to craft a powerful brand narrative:

Define Your Brand's Mission and Values

The foundation of any brand story is a clear understanding of the brand's mission and values. Why does the brand exist? What does it believe in? These core values should be woven into every aspect of the narrative, creating a sense of purpose that resonates with consumers who share similar beliefs.

Know Your Audience

Understanding the audience is critical to crafting a story that resonates. Who are they? What do they care about? What are their pain points, desires, and values? A deep understanding of the audience allows brands to tailor their stories to speak directly to their emotions and needs.

Highlight the Brand's Journey

Every brand has a story of how it started. Sharing the brand's journey, whether it's a scrappy startup story, a personal passion project, or a mission-driven cause, helps humanize the brand and make it more relatable. For example, TOMS Shoes shares the story of its founder, Blake Mycoskie, and how his travels to Argentina inspired the company's "One for One" model, where for every pair of shoes sold, a pair is donated to someone in need. This narrative gives the brand purpose and resonates with socially conscious consumers.

In today's marketing landscape, facts and figures are not enough to capture consumers' hearts. While product features and benefits are important, they often lack the emotional resonance that drives consumer behavior. Storytelling has emerged as one of the most powerful tools brands can use to engage their audience on a deeper level. Through storytelling, brands can communicate their values, mission, and personality in a way that resonates emotionally, creating memorable experiences that inspire loyalty and advocacy.

At its core, storytelling is about making a connection. Stories have been used for centuries to convey messages, share experiences, and build relationships, and in the world of marketing, this age-old tradition is more relevant than ever. Whether through advertising, content marketing, or social media, brands that tell compelling stories are more likely to build lasting relationships with their customers.

Focus on Customer Success Stories

Customer success stories are one of the most powerful forms of storytelling. Brands can create relatable and authentic narratives by highlighting real customers who have benefited from their products or services. These stories show the audience how the brand can improve their lives, making the message more tangible and impactful.

Keep It Simple and Human

The best stories are often the simplest ones. Brands don't need to overcomplicate their narratives with jargon or overly polished content. Instead, focus on telling a human story that people can connect with. Simplicity and authenticity will always resonate more than flashy, overproduced content.

Using Storytelling Across Platforms

Storytelling can be adapted to fit different marketing platforms, from social media and content marketing to advertising and in-store experiences. Here's how brands can use storytelling across various platforms:

Takeaway

In a world where consumers are bombarded with endless choices and information, storytelling has become the key to building deeper connections, standing out from the competition, and inspiring loyalty. Brands that master the art of storytelling can engage their audience on an emotional level, making their message more memorable, impactful, and authentic. Ultimately, it's not just about selling a product, it's about telling a story that people want to be a part of.

Chapter 14

The Role Of Data In Understanding And Reaching Customers

In today's digital world, data is often called the new oil. It is an invaluable resource that fuels marketing strategies, shapes customer experiences, and drives business growth. The ability to collect, analyze, and act on data has fundamentally changed how brands understand and interact with their customers. Data allows brands to deliver more relevant, meaningful experiences at every touchpoint, from personalized product recommendations to targeted advertising.

However, as data becomes more integral to marketing, it raises important questions about privacy, transparency, and ethical use. In this chapter, we'll explore how brands can leverage data to gain insights into customer behavior, personalize marketing efforts, and improve customer experiences, all while respecting privacy and building trust.

The Types of Data Brands Collect

Brands today have access to an overwhelming amount of data, often categorized into three key types: first-party, second-party, and third-party data. Each type of data serves a unique purpose and provides different insights into customer behavior.

First-Party Data

First-party data is collected directly from customers through interactions on a company's platforms. This includes website visits, app usage, purchase history, email engagement, and customer feedback. First-party data is the most valuable because it is reliable, consent-based, and provides direct insights into customer behavior.

Second-Party Data

Second-party data is shared between trusted partners. For example, if two companies have a partnership, one may share its first-party data with the other. This data type is often used to expand audience reach or gain insights into new customer segments. Second-party data remains relatively trustworthy as it originates from direct consumer relationships.

Third-Party Data

Third-party data is collected by external organizations that are not directly involved with the consumer. It is typically aggregated from multiple sources and sold to brands for marketing purposes. While third-party data can help expand audience targeting, it is often considered less reliable than first-party or second-party data. Growing concerns about consumer privacy have led to increased scrutiny of third-party data usage.

How Data Helps Brands Understand Customers

Data provides valuable insights into who customers are, what they want, and how they behave. By analyzing customer data, brands can refine their marketing strategies and product offerings to better serve their audience.

Customer Segmentation

Data enables brands to segment their audience based on demographics, interests, behaviors, and purchasing habits. Segmentation is crucial for creating targeted marketing campaigns that resonate with specific customer groups. For example, a fashion retailer might segment its audience into frequent buyers, bargain shoppers, or trend followers, tailoring messaging to each group accordingly. By understanding each segment's unique needs, brands can deliver more personalized experiences that drive engagement and conversion rates.

Behavioral Insights

Behavioral data, such as website clicks, time spent on a page, cart abandonment, and product interactions, gives brands insight into how customers interact with their platforms. This data reveals patterns in consumer behavior, helping brands identify what's working and where improvements are needed.

For example, if a high percentage of users abandon their carts at checkout, the brand can investigate whether a UX issue, pricing concern, or another factor is driving this behavior. With this data, the brand can adjust its strategy to improve the customer experience and reduce abandonment rates.

Predictive Analytics

Predictive analytics uses historical data and algorithms to forecast future customer behavior. By analyzing past purchases, website visits, or engagement with marketing content, brands can anticipate what products or services a customer might be interested in next.

For example, an e-commerce company might use predictive analytics to recommend products based on a customer's browsing or purchase history. This increases the likelihood of a purchase while enhancing the customer experience through relevant and timely recommendations.

Personalization: Using Data to Tailor Experiences

One of the most powerful uses of customer data is personalization. Personalization involves tailoring the customer experience based on preferences, behaviors, and past interactions. When done effectively, personalization can significantly boost engagement, customer satisfaction, and brand loyalty.

Personalized Product Recommendations

Many leading e-commerce platforms, like Amazon and Netflix, use data-driven personalization to offer highly relevant product or content recommendations. By analyzing browsing history, past purchases, and search behavior, these platforms suggest products or shows aligned with customer preferences.

Amazon's recommendation engine, for example, accounts for a significant portion of its sales by suggesting products customers are most likely to buy. This level of personalization not only increases sales but also enhances the shopping experience, making it more enjoyable and efficient.

Dynamic Email Marketing

Email marketing is another area where personalization can have a significant impact. Brands that segment their email lists based on customer data and send dynamic content, such as personalized product recommendations, special offers, or reminders based on customer behavior, see higher open rates and conversions.

For example, if a customer browses a product but doesn't complete the purchase, the brand can send a personalized follow-up email reminding them of the product and offering an incentive to complete the purchase. By leveraging data, brands can turn abandoned carts into completed sales and foster long-term customer relationships.

Tailored Advertising

Data-driven advertising allows brands to create highly targeted ads based on customer behavior and preferences. Platforms like Facebook and Google Ads enable brands to serve personalized ads to users based on their online activity, such as websites visited, products viewed, or items added to their cart.

Retargeting campaigns, which show ads to users who have previously interacted with the brand, are particularly effective for converting customers who may be on the fence. These ads remind customers of their previous interests and can include tailored offers to encourage a purchase.

The Ethical Use of Data and Consumer Privacy

As data becomes increasingly central to marketing, concerns about privacy and data security have grown. Consumers are more aware of how their data is being used and expect brands to be transparent about its collection, storage, and usage. Mishandling data can result in a loss of trust and significant reputational damage.

Transparency and Consent

A fundamental principle of ethical data use is transparency. Brands must clearly communicate what data they collect, how it is used, and how long it is stored. Providing customers with accessible privacy policies and allowing them to opt into data collection ensures that they remain in control of their personal information.

For example, brands that use cookies to track website activity should clearly inform users and allow them to consent to tracking. Additionally, offering an easy way for users to update or delete their data fosters trust and aligns with best practices for data privacy.

Data Security

Data breaches can have severe consequences for both consumers and brands. Ensuring customer data is securely stored and protected from unauthorized access is critical. Companies must invest in robust security measures, such as encryption, multi-factor authentication, and regular system audits to mitigate risks.

Failing to protect customer data can lead to financial penalties, legal consequences, and irreparable damage to a brand's reputation.

Privacy Laws and Regulations

Brands must comply with privacy laws and regulations, such as the General Data Protection Regulation (GDPR) in Europe and the California Consumer Privacy Act (CCPA) in the U.S. These regulations grant consumers greater control over their data and impose strict guidelines on how brands collect, store, and use personal information.

Compliance with these laws is not only a legal necessity but also a way to build consumer trust by demonstrating respect for privacy.

Balancing Personalization with Privacy

While data enables highly personalized experiences, brands must strike a balance between offering personalization and respecting privacy. Consumers value relevant, tailored interactions but want assurance that their information is protected and used responsibly. Finding this balance fosters trust and strengthens relationships with customers.

Providing Value in Exchange for Data

Customers are more likely to share their data when they perceive value in return. When consumers understand that sharing their preferences, interests, or behaviors leads to better experiences, such as personalized recommendations or exclusive offers, they are more willing to provide their information.

For example, loyalty programs often request customers' purchase history or preferences in exchange for rewards, discounts, or early access to products. These programs create a mutually beneficial relationship where customers feel they gain value in return for sharing their data.

Avoiding Over-Personalization

Excessive personalization can make consumers uncomfortable, especially if it feels intrusive. Brands must be mindful of how they use data to avoid crossing the line. For instance, retargeting ads that follow users across multiple websites or emails referencing overly specific details can make customers feel as though they are being watched.

To prevent over-personalization, brands should focus on delivering relevant experiences without making it obvious that every interaction is being tracked. Subtlety is key to maintaining consumer trust while leveraging data effectively.

Giving Customers Control

Providing customers with control over their data is essential. Allowing users to easily manage their preferences, opt out of data collection, or choose their level of personalization fosters transparency and trust. Brands that prioritize consumer control over data usage are more likely to build long-term relationships based on mutual respect.

Case Study: Spotify's Data-Driven Personalization

Spotify exemplifies how brands can use data to enhance customer experiences. The streaming platform leverages user data to create highly personalized interactions, from its Discover Weekly playlist to its year-end Spotify Wrapped campaign.

Discover Weekly is a customized playlist generated based on a user's listening habits. By analyzing preferred songs and genres, Spotify curates a unique weekly playlist tailored to each user. This data-driven personalization enhances user engagement and satisfaction.

At the end of each year, **Spotify Wrapped** provides users with a personalized summary of their listening habits, including their most-played songs, artists, and genres. This campaign is highly shareable, creating social media buzz as users post their Wrapped results. By using data to deliver personalized, engaging content, Spotify has built deep user loyalty and a strong sense of community.

Takeaway

Data is essential for understanding and reaching customers in today's digital landscape. From customer segmentation and behavioral insights to predictive analytics and personalization, data allows brands to deliver more relevant, meaningful experiences. However, with great power comes great responsibility. Brands must ensure they use data ethically, respect consumer privacy, and comply with regulations. By balancing personalization with privacy, companies can build trust, enhance customer experiences, and drive long-term loyalty.

Chapter 15

Building A Brand That Lasts: The Long Game In Customer Relationships

Building a brand that stands the test of time requires more than just clever marketing campaigns or viral moments. It demands a long-term vision, a deep understanding of customer relationships, and a commitment to continual evolution without losing the brand's core essence. In an ever-changing market, where trends and technologies shift rapidly, the brands that succeed in the long run balance consistency with adaptability.

While chasing short-term sales or capitalizing on fleeting trends may be tempting, true longevity comes from creating value over time and fostering strong, lasting customer relationships. This chapter explores the principles and strategies that help brands survive and thrive over the long term.

The Importance of Long-Term Thinking

One of the most common mistakes brands make is focusing solely on short-term gains, whether hitting quarterly revenue targets, running limited-time promotions, or chasing quick wins through viral content. While these tactics can deliver immediate results, they often come at the cost of long-term brand health. Short-term strategies may drive sales, but without a sustainable approach, they risk eroding trust, diluting brand identity, or alienating loyal customers.

Why Long-Term Thinking Matters

1. **Customer Trust Takes Time to Build**

   Trust is the foundation of any successful brand-customer relationship, and it cannot be earned overnight. Building trust requires consistent delivery of promises, transparent communication, and a commitment to customer satisfaction over time. Brands focusing on the long game prioritize trust-building interactions, understanding that trust leads to repeat business and advocacy.

2. **Brand Equity Is a Long-Term Asset**

   Brand equity refers to the value a brand holds in the eyes of consumers. This value is built over time through positive experiences, consistent messaging, and a strong reputation. Brands with high equity can command higher prices, attract loyal customers, and weather market changes more effectively than brands with little to no equity. Building brand equity requires a long-term investment in customer relationships, quality, and innovation.

3. **Sustainability vs. Trend Chasing**

   While it can be tempting to jump on the latest trends or capitalize on viral moments, brands that last focus on sustainable growth rather than short-lived fads. Trend-chasing often leads to inconsistent messaging, which can confuse or alienate customers. Instead, lasting brands focus on delivering long-term value while staying true to their core identity.

Key Strategies for Building a Brand That Lasts

Consistency in Brand Identity and Values

One of the hallmarks of long-lasting brands is their consistency. Whether it's their messaging, visual identity, or customer experience, successful brands maintain a sense of continuity that customers come to rely on. This consistency does not mean brands cannot evolve, but they must stay true to their core values and identity even as they grow and adapt.

Consistency builds trust because customers know what to expect from the brand. It also reinforces the brand's position in the market, making it easier for customers to recognize and remember it.

Example: Coca-Cola

Coca-Cola is one of the world's most iconic brands, known for its consistent messaging and visual identity. For decades, Coca-Cola has positioned itself as a symbol of happiness, refreshment, and togetherness. While the company has adapted its marketing strategies to stay relevant, it has always maintained its core values and brand messaging. The red-and-white logo, the slogan "Open Happiness," and the classic bottle design have become timeless symbols, contributing to Coca-Cola's enduring brand equity.

Customer-Centricity: Put the Customer at the Heart of Everything

Brands that last understand that their success depends on their ability to meet and exceed customer expectations. Customer-centricity means putting the customer at the heart of every decision, from product development and customer service to marketing and branding.

Long-term success comes from fostering a deep understanding of customer needs, preferences, and pain points, and continuously working to address them. Brands that prioritize customer feedback, offer personalized experiences, and provide exceptional service are more likely to build loyal, lasting relationships.

Example: Amazon

Amazon has built its empire on customer-centricity. From the start, Amazon's mission has been to be the "Earth's most customer-centric company." This philosophy drives everything from its product selection to its logistics operations. Amazon prioritizes convenience, fast delivery, and customer satisfaction, continuously using data to improve its offerings. The company's focus on the customer has helped it maintain loyalty and trust, even as it has grown into one of the largest e-commerce platforms in the world.

Innovate Without Losing Your Core

Innovation is crucial to staying relevant in a fast-changing market, but it should never come at the expense of the brand's core identity. Brands that last are those that can innovate, whether through new products, services, or business models, while maintaining a connection to what makes them unique.

Innovation should align with the brand's values and promise to customers. When innovation feels authentic and purposeful, it strengthens the brand's position rather than diluting it.

Example: Apple

Apple is a brand synonymous with innovation. From the launch of the Macintosh in the 1980s to the iPhone revolution in the 2000s, Apple has continually pushed the boundaries of technology. However, Apple's success lies in its ability to innovate while staying true to its core values of simplicity, user experience, and design. Every product Apple releases reflects these values, ensuring customers remain loyal even as the company introduces new technologies.

Adapt to Changing Market Dynamics

While consistency is important, lasting brands also know how to adapt. The market is constantly evolving due to new technologies, shifting consumer preferences, and economic forces. Brands that are unwilling or unable to adapt risk becoming irrelevant.

Adaptability doesn't mean abandoning core values but being open to change and finding ways to stay relevant. Brands that pivot, embrace new opportunities, and meet evolving customer needs are better positioned to thrive in the long run.

Example: Netflix

Netflix began as a DVD rental service, but as consumer preferences shifted toward streaming, the company quickly adapted its business model. By investing heavily in its streaming platform and original content, Netflix became an entertainment industry leader. Its ability to pivot in response to technological and consumer trends has kept the brand relevant, even as competitors like Disney+ and HBO Max entered the market.

Build a Community Around Your Brand

Brands that foster a sense of community create stronger emotional connections with customers. Communities provide customers with a space to engage with the brand, share experiences, and connect with like-minded individuals. This sense of belonging deepens loyalty and encourages advocacy.

Whether through social media groups, brand events, or loyalty programs, creating a sense of community can turn customers into lifelong fans who advocate for the brand and attract new customers.

Example: Harley-Davidson

Harley-Davidson has built one of the most loyal brand communities in the world. The Harley Owners Group (H.O.G.) connects motorcycle enthusiasts who share a passion for the brand. This community organizes rides, events, and social gatherings, giving members a sense of belonging and identity. By fostering this community, Harley-Davidson has built a fiercely loyal customer base that views the brand as more than just a product, it's a lifestyle.

Sustaining a Legacy: Brands That Stand the Test of Time

Commitment to Quality

Brands that last prioritize quality in everything they do. Quality is non-negotiable, whether in the product itself, customer service, or the overall brand experience. Consistently delivering high-quality products and experiences reinforces the brand's reputation and keeps customers returning.

Example: Rolex

Rolex is known for its commitment to craftsmanship and precision. The brand has built its reputation on the quality of its watches, which symbolize luxury and status. Rolex has remained a market leader in the luxury watch industry for over a century by maintaining the highest quality standards while innovating in watch technology and design.

Social Responsibility and Purpose

Consumers today expect brands to stand for something beyond profit. Brands that align themselves with social or environmental causes create deeper emotional connections with customers. Purpose-driven brands are more likely to build loyalty, as customers feel good about supporting companies that share their values and contribute to the greater good.

Example: Patagonia

Patagonia has built its brand around environmental activism. The company is committed to sustainability and ethical practices, from using recycled materials in its products to advocating for climate action. Patagonia's customers see the brand as a leader in environmental responsibility, and this purpose-driven approach has helped build a loyal customer base that values not just the product, but the company's mission.

The Role of Leadership in Building a Lasting Brand

Strong leadership is behind every lasting brand. Visionary leaders guide their companies with a long-term perspective, balancing innovation with stability. These leaders inspire trust, set the tone for the company's culture, and ensure that the brand remains true to its values even as it grows and evolves.

Leadership plays a critical role in shaping a brand's future. Companies with strong, purpose-driven leadership are more likely to remain relevant in the long run.

Example: Walt Disney

Walt Disney's visionary leadership made The Walt Disney Company one of the most beloved entertainment brands. His commitment to innovation, creativity, and storytelling continues to influence the company's culture and identity. Under strong leadership, Disney has expanded its reach through acquisitions like Pixar, Marvel, and Lucasfilm while maintaining the magic and family-friendly values that have defined the brand for decades.

Takeaway

Building a lasting brand requires a long-term vision, a commitment to quality, and a deep understanding of customer relationships. Brands that focus on creating lasting value, fostering trust, and staying true to their core values are more likely to thrive in an ever-changing market. While short-term gains may be tempting, brands that play the long game, by innovating, adapting, and prioritizing customer-centricity, stand the test of time.

In the end, building a lasting brand isn't just about selling a product. It's about creating an enduring legacy that resonates with customers for generations.

Chapter 16

What Is Social Selling
And Why Does It Matter?

Social selling leverages social media platforms to engage with prospects, nurture relationships, and drive sales. Unlike traditional selling techniques that rely on cold calling or hard pitches, social selling provides value, builds trust, and fosters meaningful interactions with potential customers.

With the rise of digital transformation, social selling has become a key component of modern marketing and sales strategies. As consumers increasingly spend time on social media, brands must connect with them in a way that resonates. In today's visually driven world, video is the most effective format for executing a powerful social selling strategy.

The Power of Video in Social Selling

Video content captures attention faster than text or images alone. With platforms like Instagram, TikTok, LinkedIn, YouTube, and Facebook prioritizing video content, brands that use video for social selling have a distinct advantage.

Why Video Works for Social Selling:

- **Higher Engagement** – Videos generate 1200% more shares than text and images combined.

- **Stronger Emotional Connection** – Facial expressions, tone, and storytelling build trust.
- **Better Product Demonstration** – Customers can see how products work in real-time.
- **Increased Brand Recall** – People retain 95% of a message in video form, compared to 10% from text.

When executed correctly, a social selling strategy using video can transform how brands attract, engage, and convert their audiences.

How to Execute a Social Selling Strategy with Video

1. Define Your Target Audience

Before creating videos, identify your ideal customers. Consider demographics, interests, challenges, and behaviors. Tools like **Facebook Audience Insights, LinkedIn Analytics, and Instagram's Professional Dashboard** can provide valuable data.

2. Choose the Right Platforms

Each social media platform has different audience behaviors and content preferences.

- **LinkedIn** – Best for B2B social selling with educational and thought leadership videos.
- **Instagram & TikTok** – Ideal for short, engaging, and viral-style videos.
- **Facebook & YouTube** – Perfect for longer, in-depth product demonstrations and storytelling.
- **Twitter/X** – Great for short clips and conversational engagement.

3. Create Different Types of Social Selling Videos

- **Live Videos** – Host Q&A sessions, product launches, and behind-the-scenes streams.

- **Tutorials & How-Tos** – Educate customers on how to use your product effectively.
- **Customer Testimonials** – Showcase real customers sharing their positive experiences.
- **Storytelling Videos** – Humanize your brand with compelling narratives.
- **User-Generated Content (UGC)** – Feature content created by satisfied customers.

4. Optimize Videos for Each Platform

Ensure your videos align with platform-specific guidelines. For example:

- **Instagram Reels & TikTok** – Vertical videos, 15-60 seconds, engaging hooks.
- **YouTube** – Horizontal, long-form videos (5+ minutes), detailed content.
- **LinkedIn** – Professional, value-driven, short (1-3 minutes).

5. Engage, Don't Just Sell

Social selling is about relationship-building, not hard selling. Engage with viewers by responding to comments, answering questions, and initiating discussions.

- **Ask questions at the end of your videos** to encourage interaction.
- **Reply to every comment and message** to build rapport.
- **Use storytelling instead of sales pitches** to make content feel natural and engaging.

6. Leverage Influencers and Brand Advocates

Collaborate with industry influencers, brand ambassadors, or satisfied customers who can authentically promote your brand through video.

7. Track Performance and Optimize

Analyze video performance using platform analytics. Key metrics include:

- **Views & Watch Time** – Indicates audience interest.
- **Engagement (Likes, Shares, Comments)** – Measures interaction.
- **Click-Through Rate (CTR)** – Tracks conversions.

Adjust content based on data insights to improve future videos.

Common Mistakes Brands Make in Social Selling with Video (And How to Avoid Them)

Even with a solid strategy, many brands fall into common pitfalls that hurt their social selling efforts. Here's what to avoid:

Mistake 1: Making Videos Too Salesy

⬤ **What Happens?** – Viewers feel like they're watching an ad and scroll past.

✅ **Solution:** Focus on storytelling, education, or entertainment rather than direct selling.

Mistake 2: Ignoring Video SEO

⬤ **What Happens?** – Videos don't rank, limiting visibility.

✅ **Solution:** Use keyword-rich titles, descriptions, and tags to optimize for search.

Mistake 3: Not Having a Call-to-Action (CTA)

⬤ **What Happens?** – Viewers enjoy the content but don't take action.

✅ **Solution:** Include clear CTAs like "Visit our website," "Comment below," or "DM us for more info."

Mistake 4: Poor Video Quality

⬤ **What Happens?** – Blurry visuals, bad lighting, or poor audio reduces credibility.

✅ **Solution:** Invest in a good smartphone, microphone, and proper lighting setup.

Mistake 5: Not Engaging with Viewers

⬤ **What Happens?** – Missed opportunities to build relationships and trust.

✅ **Solution:** Reply to comments, ask questions, and personalize interactions.

Mistake 6: Posting Inconsistently

⬤ **What Happens?** – Audience forgets your brand exists.

✅ **Solution:** Create a content calendar and stick to a posting schedule.

Takeaway

Social selling with video is no longer optional, it's essential. Video content increases engagement, builds trust, and helps brands connect with their audience more authentically.

By defining your target audience, choosing the right platforms, and creating engaging video content, your brand can generate leads, drive sales, and establish long-term customer relationships. Avoiding common mistakes will ensure your social selling strategy is effective and impactful.

Now, it's time to take action. Start integrating video into your social selling strategy today and watch your brand thrive!

Chapter 17

Future Marketing Trends And The Role AR, VR, AI, And Automation Will Play.

Are You Ready for the Future of Marketing?

2025 is set to be a transformative year for marketing, with cutting-edge technologies like Augmented Reality (AR), Virtual Reality (VR), Artificial Intelligence (AI), and automation playing a critical role in reshaping digital experiences. These innovations are redefining how businesses interact with customers, creating deeper and more meaningful connections. In this chapter, we'll explore how these advanced techniques can drive customer engagement and give businesses a competitive edge. Let's dive in!

The Evolution of Marketing Trends

Marketing strategies are evolving at an unprecedented pace. What worked five years ago may now be obsolete. The rise of social media, influencer marketing, and personalized experiences has significantly heightened consumer expectations. Marketers must prioritize valuable content, brand loyalty, and seamless user experiences to stay relevant.

As digital spaces become saturated with advertisements, consumers are more selective about what they engage with. To capture attention, marketers must integrate trends like video marketing, micro-moments, and interactive content. Staying updated on evolving marketing strategies and adapting to consumer behavior is essential for maintaining a competitive edge.

Artificial Intelligence in Marketing Strategies

Artificial intelligence is revolutionizing marketing by enhancing how businesses target and engage consumers. From AI-powered chatbots to predictive analytics, AI enables brands to analyze vast amounts of data, providing deep insights into consumer behavior and preferences.

- **Personalized Campaigns** – AI-driven insights allow for hyper-personalized marketing strategies that resonate with individual customers.
- **Chatbots & Virtual Assistants** – AI-powered chatbots provide 24/7 customer support, streamlining the buying process and enhancing satisfaction.
- **Predictive Analytics** – Businesses can forecast trends, optimize campaigns, and make data-driven decisions to maximize ROI.

AI is shifting marketing toward a data-driven, customer-centric approach, allowing businesses to craft highly effective strategies with minimal waste.

The Impact of Augmented and Virtual Reality on Marketing

AR and VR technologies are rapidly transforming customer engagement. These immersive experiences allow consumers to interact with brands in unprecedented ways.

- **Virtual Try-Ons** – Customers can see how clothing, accessories, or makeup will look before purchasing.
- **Immersive Brand Experiences** – Companies can create engaging virtual showrooms or interactive product demonstrations.

- **Enhanced Storytelling** – AR/VR enables brands to craft compelling narratives that resonate deeply with consumers.

As these technologies continue to evolve, they will become integral to digital marketing strategies, enhancing brand engagement and customer loyalty.

The Role of Automation in Marketing Campaigns

Automation is streamlining marketing processes, enabling teams to focus on strategy while minimizing repetitive tasks.

- **Email Marketing Automation** – Personalized email sequences based on customer behavior improve engagement and conversions.
- **Social Media Scheduling** – Automated posting ensures consistent content delivery and audience engagement.
- **AI-Driven Ad Targeting** – Machine learning optimizes ad placements and budgets for better ROI.

While automation enhances efficiency, human creativity remains essential in crafting compelling narratives that resonate with audiences.

Key Considerations for Leveraging New Technologies

Emerging technologies offer immense opportunities, but marketers must navigate them thoughtfully.

- **Data Privacy & Security** – Adhering to data protection regulations and ensuring ethical AI use is crucial.
- **Avoiding Algorithmic Bias** – AI-driven strategies must be carefully monitored to prevent bias and maintain fairness.
- **Adapting to Consumer Expectations** – As technology evolves, so do customer behaviors. Marketers must continuously reassess and refine their strategies.

By staying informed and proactive, businesses can maximize the benefits of these innovations while mitigating potential risks.

Maximizing ROI with Emerging Technologies

Harnessing emerging technologies effectively can significantly enhance marketing performance and ROI. Here's how:

- **Leverage AI & Machine Learning** – Use data-driven insights to create highly targeted campaigns.
- **Invest in AR/VR Experiences** – Enhance customer engagement through immersive storytelling.
- **Automate Strategically** – Utilize automation to improve efficiency while maintaining a human touch.
- **Monitor & Optimize Performance** – Regularly analyze key metrics to refine strategies and maximize effectiveness.

Businesses that embrace these advancements will position themselves ahead of the competition, fostering deeper customer relationships and driving long-term success.

Takeaway: Embrace the Future of Marketing

Marketing is evolving at an extraordinary pace, and businesses must stay ahead of the curve to maintain a competitive edge. By integrating AI, AR, VR, and automation into their strategies, marketers can create more engaging, efficient, and impactful campaigns.

Now is the time to assess your company's position in the shifting marketing landscape. How will you leverage these technologies to drive growth and stay ahead of the competition? The future of marketing is here, are you ready to embrace it?

Let's get started!

Chapter 18

Playing The Long Game

As we conclude this exploration of modern consumerism and brand-building, one fundamental truth emerges: long-term success depends on building relationships, not just making sales. Today's consumers are more informed, empowered, and discerning than ever. To thrive in this evolving landscape, brands must stay true to their core identity, foster trust through authenticity, and adapt to meet changing customer needs.

Throughout this book, we've examined how brands can connect with consumers by leveraging authenticity, social media, influencers, user experience, and data-driven insights. These tools, when used effectively, enable companies to create lasting and meaningful relationships with their customers. However, at the heart of every great brand lies a crucial principle: it's not just about what you sell, it's about how you make people feel.

Industry leaders like Apple, Starbucks, Patagonia, and Nike have demonstrated that consistency, innovation, and customer-centricity are the cornerstones of enduring success. They prove that by prioritizing both functional value and emotional connection, brands can cultivate relationships that withstand the test of time.

In a marketplace where trust and loyalty must be earned, brands must recognize one essential reality: if customers don't believe in your brand, you don't matter. Success lies in understanding their journey, addressing their needs, and delivering authentic, human-centric experiences that resonate on a deeper level. The brands that master this approach will not only thrive but also leave a lasting legacy for generations to come.

About the Author

Phil Masiello is a visionary leader with over two decades of experience in e-commerce, marketing, and startups. As the founder of CrunchGrowth, he has made a lasting impact on business strategy and digital commerce. His entrepreneurial journey began at 27, backed by an MBA in Marketing and Finance, which has been a driving force in his success.

From pioneering e-commerce in the meal industry with The Daily Market to co-founding Raw Essentials Skin Care with Carol Alt, Phil has consistently demonstrated strategic innovation. His expertise spans brand strategy and digital marketing across consumer product categories, including food, fashion, beauty, and personal care.

As a founder and CEO, he has built disruptive business models that merge emerging technologies with evolving consumer lifestyles. His ability to craft effective digital and social strategies has propelled brand recognition and accelerated revenue growth. His ventures, such as 800razors.com, showcase his creative use of PR to scale, while CrunchGrowth is recognized for its cost-effective and innovative methods in driving sales for their brand clients, particularly in the consumer products categories.

Phil's expertise in multi-channel customer acquisition has helped brands expand rapidly while maintaining efficiency. As a specialist in direct to consumer selling methods, he is deeply involved in financial planning, sales, marketing, and operational strategy for multi-platform brand development.

Beyond his business ventures, Phil shares his knowledge as the host of *Crunching Your Growth* on e360tv, where he engages with industry experts to inspire and educate the next generation of entrepreneurs.

His specialties include e-commerce, brand development, digital and social media marketing, branding and identity, retail, infomercials, television shopping channels, and direct-response TV. His career exemplifies transformative thinking and the ability to thrive in the ever-evolving digital marketplace.

ISBN: 979-8-9882053-2-6

Appsydo, LLC

www.ingramcontent.com/pod-product-compliance
Lightning Source LLC
Chambersburg PA
CBHW060039210326
41520CB00009B/1186